COUNTRY LAWYER, LAST OF A DYING BREED

COUNTRY LAWYER, LAST OF A DYING BREED

Also, Confidations, A Collection of Loveable Client Malaprops
And a Country Lawyer's Collection of Aphorisms For A Worthy Life

JOHN E. TYO, ESQ.

PALMETTO
PUBLISHING
Charleston, SC
www.PalmettoPublishing.com

Copyright © 2024 by John E. Tyo, Esq.

All rights reserved

No portion of this book may be reproduced, stored in a retrieval system, or transmitted in any form by any means–electronic, mechanical, photocopy, recording, or other–except for brief quotations in printed reviews, without prior permission of the author.

Hardcover ISBN: 979-8-8229-6116-6
Paperback ISBN: 979-8-8229-5881-4

To all those who respect The Rule of Law

CONTENTS

INTRODUCTION — XI
How The Book Is Organized. xii
The Country Law Office xiii
My Hopes For The Book xiv

THE CIVIL CASES/MATTERS — 1
First, The Civil Cases/Matters. 1
Grandma Saves The House 1
The Granny Goes To Jail Law 3
Granny's Lawyer Goes To Jail 5
Two Brothers and The Lost Farm 5
Brother's Keeper. 6
The Brother Who Wanted It All. 9
Father of the Year. 13
Egregious Conduct 17
Ricky 20
"Here's Your Newborn Child". 22
"I'll Support The Child Because I'm A Nice Guy". 23
When To Fire A Client 25
The Best Answer Ever 28
The Worm Turned. Twice. 31

ADVANCE PLANNING — 34
The Perfect Will Gone Wrong 34
Old Wills Never Die 36
Clara 39
Gifts From The Heart. 40
"No! I Won't Go!". 42

REAL ESTATE — 44

Housewarming Gifts To Mega Insurance Companies 44
Foreclosure: Have A Group Hug, Sing Kubaya And Give
Him A Deed. 46
How To Keep The Family Camp In The Family; Or Not 50
You Better Go Get A Good Lawyer 51
The Six By Twelve Driveway 52
You Can't Make This Stuff Up 53
There's A Divinity That Shapes Our Ends 55
A Final Word About Real Estate 56

JUDGES — 58

How To Make A Judge Angry 58
An Early Lesson. 61
It's Not Easy Being A Judge 64
But Sometimes It Can Be Fun 68
Take Him Into Custody! Please!. 70

LAWYERS — 71

Adversaries Can Be Friends 71
"Ready If Not Reached" 74
Nightmares 75
Deadline. 76
The Cold Clutches Of IRS 78
The Missing Security Interest Filing 79
Lunch With Bob 81
CLEAR THE COURTROOM! 81
Ham and Eggers 82

PARALEGALS — 84

"How Can I Hold You?" 84
Like Drill Sergeants. 86
I Was Never Alone 87

ON THE WAY TO SHORTSVILLE — 88
Early Career In A Nutshell 88

THE CRIMINAL MATTERS — 90
The White Hat 90
The Black Hat 92
Can Nags Be Racehorses? 92
Duck 94
Did I Have Anything To Drink At Lunch, Mary? 95

THE ASSIGNED FELONY CASES — 100
Assigned Counsel - The Black Hat 100
First Assigned Felony Case: A Murder 101
A Digression: The Importance of Defense Counsel 104
The Accidentally Perfect Shot 107
Vicious Evil, Pure and Simple 108
The Teacher 110
The Killing of Nancy Davis 114
The end of tranquility; A dark, hidden secret 116
Conscience 116
The first unimaginable coincidence 118
Flight 118
Paranoia 119
The second, unthinkable, coincidence 119
Blood tests 120
Notebook; The Blue Blanket 120
What Is Suppression? 121
The Suppression Hearing 123
New Lawyer, Trials, Conviction 125
"I Did It" 126
Fast Forward to 1990 126
He Fell Asleep On The Toilet? 127
Ineffective Assistance Of Counsel 128

Fidel Castro's Ambassadors 132
The Tail of the Whale. 135

MISCELLANEOUS ODDS 'N ENDS — 138

Um..... Is That A Jetliner?. 138
Maybe It's Not So Bad In Siberia 140
The Lawsuit I Couldn't Afford. 141
Safety Harnesses In The Showers? 144
Glimpses Of A Country Law Office. 145
Treasures Other Than Gold 150

CONFIDATIONS TO A COUNTRY LAWYER — 153

Medicine. 153
Possible Litigation. 154
Marital Bliss. 155
Criminal Law 155
Strategy 157
Etiquette. 157
Relationships 157
Finance. 158
Communication. 158
Family 159
Organization 159
Real Estate. 160
Protocol and Procedure 160
Clarity 161
Personal Recommendations 162
Common Courtesy. 162
Sex 162
Secretarial Skills 163
Letter writing skills. 163
Logic 163
Resolve. 164
Geography. 164

A COUNTRY LAWYER'S FAVORITE APHORISMS — 165

INTRODUCTION

This book is a collection of law office stories occurring over a period of my fifty-five years as a country lawyer. They are true stories told in this book not as the product of a recent review of files, most of which have been shredded, but as the recollection of them. None of the stories are fiction, though if the actual events could be played back on videotape, one would see instances in the book where approximations serve to round out the narrative.

In a perfect world, a young lawyer expecting to write a book five decades into the future would plan for it by preserving the files, the documents and notes summarizing the salient facts of the cases. But there's no time for it. No two days in a country law office are alike. And every day brings a constellation of activities: phone calls, e-mails, client appointments, walk-ins, correspondence, document preparation, paralegal conferences, closings, court appearances, legal filings....

So, on any one of such busy days the young lawyer would only see the trees in his future book, not the forest. Only at the end of his career, looking backward, would he see the forest, and in it, some, but certainly not all, of the trees. So it is with this book. Over time the decades compress today's events into something like entries in a computer hard disk; sometimes, but not always, retrievable. For the most part, the absolute clarity of today's events yields to a misty reflection of them.

So, please take these stories for what they are: imperfect recollections of things past and recalled through the filter of time. In a sense, these chronicles are a mile wide, but in many cases only a few feet deep. Still, they give the tone and flavor of a country law office.

The cadence of the stories is the beating hearts of the clients who turned to us when they needed someone to listen, someone to help, and more than anything, someone to care.

For the most part pseudonyms are used, with certain exceptions. No attempt has been made to order the stories chronologically.

HOW THE BOOK IS ORGANIZED

One of the good things about a country law general practice is that you never know what's coming through the door. The kinds of legal matters that clients bring in run the gamut, from real estate to wills and estates, to family matters good and bad, to adoptions, foreclosures, lawsuits. Every day is something new; no two days in fifty years are the same.

The following sampling of civil matters gives us an insight into the amazing variety and diversity that make a country practice interesting and rewarding. Along with the cases there are vignettes of clients, lawyers, judges and juries.

These are followed by a brief history of how I came to be a country lawyer.

Next, a variety of criminal cases, some with a little humor and some shrouded in darkness.

Next, some of the miscellaneous odds 'n ends in a country law office.

Then, "Confidations To A Country Lawyer", a collection of loveable malaprops from clients over the decades. Finally, a compilation of my favorite aphorisms, which I consider words for a worthy life.

THE COUNTRY LAW OFFICE

Nationally, just two percent of attorneys are country lawyers. I call us "The Last of a Dying Breed". According to a 2019 New York State Bar Association study, just three percent of the 183,000 lawyers in New York State practice in rural areas. And a 2020 American Bar Association study calls such areas "legal deserts", where rural Americans are underserved, a threat to access to justice.

There are no high-rise country law offices, no glamorous interior-decorated gleaming glass office enclosures, no thirty-seat walnut conference tables. Office fashion often looks like jeans.

There's a saying that the justice courts are closest to the people. The same can be said about country law offices. They are usually located on the main street of a village, highly visible, approachable and accessible. The lawyers usually live in the community and are often active in civic matters. Casual contacts between them and clients, community members, are frequent at local stores, the post office, the park, the gas station, the school.

The office paralegals also usually live in the community, and while they aren't paid as much as those in urban areas, they don't have far to drive to work, and they don't usually have to pay for parking. Their work is close to their families; over the years, they raise children, and, later, provide care for parents. And because underneath it all life's undercurrent flows, the paralegals in a small country law office are likely to act like sisters, not rivals; they cover for each other when life events come to the fore.

The warm core of a country law office feels a lot like family. Many times over decades one generation of clients carries over to a second, or even third, generation.

When you walk into a country law office, chances are someone knows who you are; it is one of the very few places left in an impersonal, mistrustful and artificially intelligent world where the welcome is real, warm and sincere.

Make no mistake: country lawyers are not hicks; they are not using ribbon manual typewriters or mimeograph machines. Out of necessity, country law offices today are just as high-tech as their urban counterparts.

But it isn't the tech that makes the country law office special.

It's the heart.

MY HOPES FOR THE BOOK

I hope my readers find this book interesting and informative, and that it speaks of the people and things that are in many ways closest to us in our daily lives.

I hope that if this book finds its way into the hands of young people thinking of a career in law, it will encourage them to consider a rural law practice. The wondrous scope and variety of the matters that come into a country law practice, along with the close relationship between client and law office will perhaps be appealing to readers in this increasingly impersonal and remote world we live in.

If so, perhaps the Country Lawyer will *not* be the Last of a Dying Breed.

And above all, it is my hope that all my readers will come away with assurance that the Rule of Law is an engine of order and good in the world, and that, in truth, it is crucial to the well being of our society.

THE CIVIL CASES/MATTERS

FIRST, THE CIVIL CASES/MATTERS

The book is divided in to two main categories of what lawyers call "matters". Those are civil matters and criminal matters.

The following civil cases give us an insight in to the variety that makes a country practice interesting and rewarding.

Very often I would say to a client: "You know, people think real estate (for example) is boring, but sometimes it can be quite thrilling."

Boring? Not so much! Most are stories about the things closest to us, things we can relate to in our daily lives.

GRANDMA SAVES THE HOUSE

As is often the case, parents, and especially an elderly parent who has lost a spouse, considers transferring the house to a child or children, reserving a "life use" in the property. The child or children have an interest called "the remainder". As long as the parent is alive, he or she can occupy the house; or even move out and rent it out, keeping the rents. When the parent passes, the remainder interest becomes a full-blown fee interest owned solely by the child/children. It is instant and automatic; no lawyers, no courts, no expense. The deed has already been recorded.

That's what Grandma Alice did. She transferred the title to her house to her son, Billy, reserving a life use to herself.

But there was a problem, something Grandma did not know. Well, two problems, actually. First, what Grandma did not know was that at the time Billy took title to the house, he owed $40,000 to IRS, and it had taken a judgment. He never told his mother, and immediately upon Billy taking title, the IRS lien attached to the house. Not physically, and no judgment/lien measures were undertaken by IRS. But the lien would stand out like a bright red flag in any future title transaction, such as the sale of the house or a mortgage loan. There could be no better example of a cloud on title.

And the second problem? Billy died young. His interest in the house passed to his estate, subject, of course, to the IRS lien. In the absence of proceedings in Surrogate's Court, the estate is in Never-Never Land.

True, Grandma owned the life use, which could not be defeated by the IRS lien, so she could stay in the house for the rest of her life. But she wanted to transfer the house to Billy's son, her grandson, Will. If she did, though, the IRS lien would travel with that conveyance, and Will's interest would be subject to the IRS lien. He would never be able to mortgage or sell the house without paying off the lien.

What to do?

Grandma consulted Jack Schuppenhauer, Esq., a fine lawyer in Canandaigua. He called me with a plan. Lawyers will sometimes call another lawyer and say, "Can I run something by you?" Jack's plan on behalf of Grandma was to bring suit against Billy's estate *to set aside the deed he received from Grandma on the basis of fraud in the inducement.* Had Billy told her about the IRS lien, she never would have conveyed the house to him; but he didn't, to everyone's detriment. Jack asked me to represent the estate, and I agreed. The plan was that I would appear in the lawsuit on behalf of the estate, and would not oppose it.

Jack commenced suit; I appeared and like a lamb, didn't oppose it.

The Court ruled equitably, in Grandma's favor, setting aside the deed. So, it was as if it never happened, which also meant that the IRS lien could not attach. Once the deed was set aside, Billy's estate no longer owned the house; title reverted to Grandma, and the IRS lien would not affect her title.

Grandma had saved the house; well, actually, Grandma's lawyer saved the house. And once the judgment setting aside the deed was filed, Grandma transferred the house to her grandson, Will, again reserving a life use.

Returning to Square One was a just result for Grandma. As we will see elsewhere in this book, IRS can always find other targets, myself being one of them.

THE GRANNY GOES TO JAIL LAW

In this case, we look at the biggest threat to Mom and Dad's estates: the costs associated with nursing homes. All their assets can be at risk in the event of a lengthy stay. Estimates of the average stay are all over the map, but one National Institute of Health puts it at 1.37 years the National Center For Assisted Living puts it as 835 days.

According to the New York State Partnership for Long Term Care, the average cost in a skilled nursing facility in the Rochester area, which includes Ontario County, is $441 *per day*, or $160,965 per year. At 1.37 years, it's $220,522. Either sum is likely to wipe out Mom and Dad's equity in the house. It is said that before World War II, we were a nation of savers; post WWII, for many of us the most significant asset we have is our home.

True, when the first spouse enters extended care, calculations are done to allow the so-called "community spouse" to remain at home with enough financial resources to sustain his/her former lifestyle. But when the "institutionalized spouse" passes, all the assets pass to the "community spouse", and if that spouse also enters a nursing home, most, if not all, of the couple's assets will be expended for his or her care.

In anticipation of this, over the decades lawyers advised many clients to transfer their house to their children, reserving a life estate to themselves. For the most part it is the asset they most wish to pass along to their family, and the most feasible transfer. The majority of clients lack cash assets to transfer, which would leave them insufficient funds for their needs.

This plan always entailed at least two discussions, and, often, further discussions with the children.

What were we actually doing? Well, if we conveyed the "remainder" interest in the house to the children, then after a "five-year lookback period" the value of the house (except for the much smaller value of the retained life estate) could not be included in the couple's assets, meaning that value could not be, in effect, attached by the nursing home. And that meant that in the absence of cash funds the likely source of funding for the nursing home was Medicaid.

A few decades ago Congress passed a law providing that the *transfer of assets to children was illegal*; Mom and Dad should not be able to pauperize themselves, passing the expense for their care along to the government. It came to be known as "*The Granny Goes to Jail Law*". This 1990s law originally made it a *federal criminal act* if a person made any transfers that intentionally resulted in Medicaid eligibility. Under Medicaid laws, there is a *presumption of guilt* that if a Medicaid applicant made an uncompensated transfer or gift within a period of time before one files a Medicaid application (usually five years on many Medicaid programs), then it is *presumed it was purposefully done to get public benefits*. Under that original law the Medicaid applicant could have prison time in addition to being ineligible for Medicaid.

Advocates for the elderly went wild, causing such a public outcry that the law was amended to eliminate criminality and disqualification of the Medicaid benefit solely by reason of the exchange of information.

Granny would not go to jail.

But.............her lawyer would.

GRANNY'S LAWYER GOES TO JAIL

After the amendment to keep Granny out jail passed, Congress changed one of the provisions of the law to make it a federal crime (felony or misdemeanor fine up to $25,000 and prison term up to five years or both) for an individual, *for a fee, to counsel or assist clients how to dispose of assets to keep them safe from the costs associated with nursing homes.*

Under the new law, any advisor (i.e., accountant, financial advisor, planner, or attorney) who received payment for transfer planning, *could then be subject to criminal charges.*

As appealing as was the idea of jailing lawyers, it wasn't long before the New York State Bar Association sued and successfully obtained an injunction in New York against enforcement of the law. It argued that the law violated the First Amendment as it regulates and has a chilling effect on free speech. Janet Reno, who was then serving as U.S. Attorney General, agreed that the law was "plainly unconstitutional under the First Amendment."

Nobody went to jail.

The moral of the story: don't mess with old people.

TWO BROTHERS AND THE LOST FARM

This case exemplifies the sweet side of human nature. No surprise it would involve farmers.

Mom and Dad owned two farms they had worked all their lives. Their two sons, both married with families, worked side by side with them their entire working lives.

As Mom and Dad were aging, they decided to transfer title to the sons during their lifetimes for the two-fold reasons that they would be able to avoid probate, and they would, in effect, "shovel out" the value of the farms so that after five years those values would be safe from nursing home expense. They did reserve a life use in both farms.

The deeds, prepared by another lawyer, ran to the two sons together, as "*joint tenants with right of survivorship*". In retrospect, this was a mistake, with certainly unintended consequences. With joint tenancy, on the death of one of the joint tenants the other owns the whole and the departed, nothing.

We always took great care with this, and advised our clients that joint tenancy was like Russian roulette. We always pointed out the difference between joint tenancy and so-called "*tenancy in common*", where on the death of one tenant *his interest passes to his heirs.*

Wouldn't you know it? With no changes in the titles to the farms, one son died, and on his death his interest passed entirely to his brother. The deceased son's family was left with nothing for their efforts over the decades.

Now, farmers seem to have an earth-bound sense of what is right, and what isn't. It's almost as though they can *feel* what is right with their calloused hands, and sense it with their hearts. It's as though they know the natural order of things.

And so it was that when the surviving brother came to our office he wanted a deed to transfer one of the farms to his deceased brother's surviving spouse and children.

It was one of those things where you say to yourself at the end of the day: *it was a good day, and I'm glad I am a lawyer.*

I don't recall whether it was springtime, but it seemed like it.

BROTHER'S KEEPER

Lest we dismiss the topic of nursing home costs without examining their impact, we turn to our client, Dale, whose brother, Arnold, had about

$400,000 in assets, including investment accounts and three parcels of real estate.

Arnold was not married and had no children, but did have several nephews and nieces.

Before the brother entered a nursing home, Dale discussed the costs with him, telling him that all his assets were at risk for his care should he find it necessary to have long-term nursing home assistance. The Medicaid rules provide that when assessing an applicant's financial eligibility for Medicaid, he or she must have limited resources, and any excess resources must be *spent down* before qualifying for assistance. To put it bluntly, Arnold was a sitting duck.

Dale told his brother that if he transferred assets to his nephews and nieces *at least five years before he applied for Medicaid's assistance* in paying for a nursing home, the transferred assets would not be considered as assets for his care. In other words, they would be safe.

In response to this discussion, Arnold did take action: he *added the names* of several of the nieces and nephews to his investment accounts, *as joint tenants with right of survivorship. But Arnold's name remained on the accounts* together with the nieces and nephews so they would all be joint tenants. If Arnold were to die, the accounts would automatically pass to the nieces or nephews.

How'd that work out?

Not so well. The Medicaid rules provide that for jointly-owned personal property, such as bank accounts, CDs, and brokerage accounts, *the entire balances of such accounts are attributable to the applicant and subject to being spent down, unless it can be proven that the other joint owner made a financial contribution to the account, in which case that portion of the account will be disregarded.*

Such was not the case with Arnold, whose nephews and nieces had contributed nothing to the accounts.

Dale asked me to hold his brother's money in trust. Over a period of a few years, Dale and I presided over the demise of *all* of Arnold's $400,000 assets. This was not an inevitability; had Arnold retained some of his assets to live on, and re-titled the rest, *outright* to the nephews and nieces and *not as joint tenants* at least five years before entering the nursing home, those assets would have been beyond the reach of Medicaid. But such a transfer is a Hobson's choice: yes the assets are preserved for the family, but the donor, Arnold, loses control of the money when he divests himself of it.

I hasten to add that I had a few clients whose attitude was: "I came into this world with nothing, and if I leave it with nothing because I paid my own way, so be it. I don't want the government to have to pay for my care." These clients were in the distinct minority; most clients attitude was: "I worked for my whole life. I would like to be able to pass something along to my kids, and I don't want it all going to a nursing home." Their attitude was buttressed by the fact that the expense of care, seemingly like everything else, had skyrocketed.

I always had the highest regard for our clients, who for the most part were hardworking, honest and humble. Many told me that if the cost of their care was reasonable, they would be more hesitant to pass the cost to the government. But the thought that their life's energies could be lost in a single year in a nursing home was daunting.

A dilemma: Isn't one of the functions of government to care for us when we are old?

On the other hand, doesn't the government pay for enough, and should, say, a millionaire be able to foist the cost of his or her care to the government while keeping all assets?

What would you do?

THE BROTHER WHO WANTED IT ALL

Here's a case that appeals to a country lawyer's sense of justice.

In 2018 a father died leaving a son and three daughters. He left no will.

The three daughters came in to see me. They related that their brother had gone to Surrogate's Court without an attorney and had gotten himself appointed Administrator of the father's estate. This would mean he would be in charge, and conferred legal authority on him to administer all estate assets.

At the time of his death the father had owned, among other things, a parcel of land on which there was a woodland house, partially constructed, but mostly finished. Upon his appointment as estate representative, the brother proceeded to have an attorney prepare a deed to the real estate in which he *conveyed the property to himself with no consideration*; meaning that he paid the estate nothing for the conveyance. The attorney had certainly not been informed of the background, and had not deliberately or knowingly helped perpetrate a fraud. The brother also had disposed of other tangible non-real estate assets, keeping the proceeds to himself.

The three sisters had no money for legal fees and disbursements; they were, like so many people, scraping by in their own lives.

They needed help.

Now, there are certain cases that make your blood boil; for me, this was one of them. I told the sisters I would look into the matter, which I did. The first and obvious way to verify what the sisters had told me was to examine the Surrogate Court records and then deed recordings. Both quickly established the truth about what the sisters had said. When I saw the court appointment and the deed whereby the brother had, indeed, acting as the estate representative, conveyed the property to himself, paying nothing into the estate, I decided I had to get involved.

I got on My High Horse.

When a person dies without a will, or *intestate*, three basic events come into play. First, since there is no will, no one is appointed *executor* or *executrix*. And without a will the decedent has left no instructions as to how to divide his or her assets. If no one does anything regarding the estate, then everything goes into limbo. In such situations certain persons can apply to be appointed *administrator* or *administratrix* of the estate. It is called *intestate administration*.

Secondly, whoever is appointed administrator has authority to deal in the assets of the estate, but acts as a *fiduciary*, meaning that the assets are not treated as his own; they are the assets of the estate. A fiduciary has the duty to identify estate assets, to preserve them, to consolidate them, to pay legitimate debts of the decedent, to sell them in an appropriate situation and to hold the net proceeds for the benefit of the beneficiaries of the estate. In other words the administrator has a *duty of loyalty*, to regard the funds coming into his hands as belonging to the estate, which ultimately means, those persons legally entitled to those assets.

New York law provides that in the absence of a will a person's assets pass to his or her next of kin in a certain order of priority. In this case, since the decedent's spouse had predeceased him, the estate was to pass to the four children in equal shares.

Thirdly, the administrator has a duty to account for all assets coming in to his possession, for all debts paid and for the net proceeds. Then, with the Court's permission, to distribute the net proceeds to the persons entitled to them.

Clearly, the brother had acted in his own interest in derogation of his duty to his sisters; in doing so, he had violated every fundamental rule of estate administration.

I immediately knew that in a perfect world we would have a battery of lawyers to attain justice for the sisters, because looking ahead, I saw the need for several legal actions:

- we had to go to *Surrogate's* Court with a petition to revoke the brother's so-called Letters of Administration;
- at the same time, we needed to have one or more of the sisters petition the court for appointment as administratrix;
- once we had our administratrix, we needed to commence an action in *Supreme* Court to rescind the deed from the estate to the brother;
- once we achieved that, we needed to wrest possession and control of the real estate from the brother; that meant an eviction proceeding in *Town* Court to put the estate in possession of the property;
- once we did that, we needed to engage a realtor to sell the property
- after the sale we would need, ironically, to file an accounting in Surrogate's Court so the brother could see what we had done and receive whatever his rightful share of the estate might be.

It was going to be a challenge; it was going to require a great deal of my time and effort. A lawyer would say to another lawyer: "You're making a career out of this case?"

But it was what justice required. None of the actions outlined above could be skipped.

I took it on with no advance fees or disbursements, such as filing fees, deferring the legal fees and advancing the disbursements until we assumed control of the real estate, and could sell it. Meanwhile, I secured insurance on the real estate, and paid the premiums for it. A no-no, but necessary, and not easy, since the real estate was unoccupied.

This case would be an odyssey.

We filed our petitions in Surrogate's Court. The brother was absolutely uncooperative, even to the point of making it difficult for us to give notice of the proceedings to him; every time we had a court appearance I had to arrange for personal service of the papers forty miles away in another county. Service would be arranged through that county's sheriff's office.

Once we obtained service, the brother, who had not retained an attorney (which made it difficult to discuss anything), demanded a hearing on the issue of revocation of his Letters. Every time he appeared in court he said the same thing: his actions were based on the fact that he helped the father build the house; and he was overcome by grief, whatever that meant in context.

We had the hearing. The judge was unpersuaded by the brother's whines. His letters were revoked and one of my clients was appointed administratrix.

Then, on to Supreme Court. I prepared a Summons and Complaint in an action to determine the title to real estate, served the papers, got a court date, served the brother; again, he wanted a hearing, without retaining counsel.

We had that hearing and obtained an order rescinding his deed and restoring title to the estate.

Next came the hard part: *eviction in Town Court* (see below; evictions aren't easy). More court appearances, but eventually, an order awarding possession ot the property to the estate. The brother had exhibited threatening behavior, not to mention a drumbeat of insistence that he was the true owner of the property, continuing and repeating the same claims he had made in Surrogate's and Supreme Court.

When after several evening Town Court appearances I obtained a Warrant of Eviction, I had to arrange for the Ontario County Sheriff to serve it. We served it, giving the brother the required notice to vacate the property on a given date. He refused. So, because we had concerns that there could be violence, and because the sisters had seen a rifle on the property, and because when on one occasion we were subjected to a rant when we visited the property, I requested the Sheriff's Office to enforce the brother's removal. On the appointed day, *six* deputy sheriffs appeared, and for the first time we took possession of the property!

We listed the property for sale and eventually sold it with the help of a dedicated realtor who trudged up the long snowbound driveway. Following the sale, I prepared an accounting for Surrogate's Court. In it, I proposed offsets sufficient to eliminate the brother's share to compensate the sisters for the brother's malfeasance.

We sold the property for $148,936. After deducting legitimate debts, insurance, taxes, court filing fees, service of process, legal fees and other expenses, we showed a net of $87,421.71.

In our accounting, our proposal for a surcharge against the brother's share was substantial enough that it more than offset his share entirely. As required, we served a copy of our Judicial Settlement petition and formal Accounting on the brother, but he defaulted in appearing. The sister who had faithfully served as Administratrix received over $6,500 for her commissions and each of the three sisters received a share of over $26,800.

It was hard-won, but in the end justice was served. I got off My High Horse and went back to work on something else.

FATHER OF THE YEAR

No question; this was the most salacious case of my career. And one where I was able to produce the most unlikely witness; but one where best efforts ended in heartbreak.

That it was a custody case, and the only case in fifty-five years that brought me to tears at its conclusion, makes it unforgettable.

Grandma and Grandpa lived in Phelps, New York with their grandson, whom I'll call Timmy, age five.

They came to me asking that I help them obtain custody of Timmy, who had been living in their home for about the last two years. After they related the unbelievable history of the matter to me, I prepared a custody petition, which had to be served out-of-state under a uniform multi-state long-arm statute in custody matters.

Timmy's father, whom I'll call Mike, was Grandma and Grandpa's *son*, who lived in a southern state. The child's mother, whom I'll call Sherry, also lived out of state. Georgia, as I recall.

"So," I asked, "how did you come to have Timmy?" My clients responded that their daughter-in-law, Sherry, brought him to them.

When I asked why, their answer shocked me as did no other case I ever had in Family Court.

Before Timmy was born, Mike, who, though he was able-bodied, was self-centered and lazy, approached *his wife*, Sherry, with a proposal.

He would pimp her out, for money, and they would live on that. She was young (twenties) and very attractive. Whether or not she was under an undue influence, or drugs, or some other personal deficit, she agreed!

Mike *arranged assignations* for Sherry, and actually *drove her to them*. And, incredibly, on some occasions he went with her *for photographs*.

Now all this is very sad; one wonders what could bring a couple, especially such a young couple, so low.

But if you have any belief or faith in redemption, for Sherry it was here, for reasons I'll explain.

Grandma and Grandpa related that Sherry had left Mike a couple of years after she gave birth to Timmy, and she brought the child to Grandma and Grandpa, thinking that was best for him until she could reorganize her life. She was living in Georgia, and hoped to find good employment and a male companion who would treat her with love and respect. (Later, she would).

As we waded through the pre-hearing court appearances, Mike appeared, with counsel. He countered Grandma and Grandpa's petition with one of his own: he wanted custody. To read his petition, one would think he was about to receive a Congressional Medal of Freedom for Father of the Year. He had reformed, had a good-paying job in sales, a nice place to live. Best of all, he alleged, he loved his son and was prepared to, um, actually *support* him (somehow, it had dawned on him that he ought to participate in the inconvenient financial aspects of fatherhood).

Pardon my sarcasm; Mike never made my list of people I admire.

Facing a hearing, I told my clients we would have trouble. "How can we prove Mike's unfitness by showing all the things he did to Sherry? It will all be hearsay, and we won't be able to get it into evidence."

"*Not if she testifies*," they said.

I replied: "What woman would travel from Georgia to a New York courtroom to debase herself with her testimony, to open all the old wounds, to expose herself and her history to others in a most embarrassing way?" I had no hope that Sherry would agree to come here to testify.

"Call her," they said; and they gave me her phone number. I called her and left a message, telling her who I was and why I was calling. I asked that she return my call.

Now, I will remember this as long as I live: a day or so later, as I was driving back to Shortsville from a court appearance in Wayne County, my cell phone rang. I remember as if it was yesterday, the exact spot where I pulled over to take the call.

It was Sherry.

"*I will be there*," she said. Any lawyer who has ever tried a case is completely reliant on the ability to identify witnesses, to contact them, to request their testimony, to try to convince those who are reluctant to appear, and to hope that at the appointed day they will.

Sherry did, and it was an epic hearing. She told the whole story, and *she brought some of the photos*, (nude scenes, compromising positions, basic pornography) which we introduced into evidence. I'm probably a soft touch, but despite this, I felt a warm redemptive breeze throughout her testimony. I've always believed it possible that one could regain one's dignity, could atone for past transgressions; could shine light where there had been only darkness. *All who wander are not lost.* I believe that (in select cases). Sherry was the physical embodiment of it; a kind of deliverance from her sorrowful past.

She testified openly, honestly, without minimizing her own conduct. Too, her testimony was hopeful: she expressed the hope that she would soon be able to have custody of Timmy, and felt that with her new life she had a chance. Overall, she made it clear what kind of man Mike was and clearly expressed concern over the values he would pass along to his son should he gain custody.

Grandma and Grandpa also testified, expressing their heartfelt wishes to keep Timmy, and relating how they provided care for him, supported him, protected and loved him.

But despite all this, the Court awarded custody to Mike on the rationale that a child should be with a biological parent, rather than his grandparents. The Court was persuaded that Mike could parent the child; his reformation was such that he deserved the chance. (Oh, spare me!)

After the court appearance, hugging Grandma and Grandpa in the hallway, we cried. The stoic, professional, unflappable lawyer's demeanor was gone. We had come so far.....

I've run into Grandpa a few times in the last few years; he always says: "Bless you, John" and it always moves me.

Many of a lawyer's cases disappear into the fog of time; the lawyer's plight is the need, always, to move on, to look forward to the next case, the next challenge. To do else is regression. If you are always looking backward, living in the past, the cases you lost will haunt you.

But I've often wondered how Timmy has made out. He's probably eighteen or nineteen now. I hope he'll chart his own course.

And I pray he'll see his Mom often.

EGREGIOUS CONDUCT

When I started practicing law in 1967 divorce matters were still in The Dark Ages.

New York law allowed but one ground for divorce: adultery. You can call me "liberal", but if events overtook a married couple and they determined it best that they separate and divorce, the worst possible way to go about it would be to require proof of unfaithfulness. That is especially true where there were children; an unseemly allegation of marital betrayal made a difficult situation worse. (And, by the way, I believe there were many cases where adultery was no more than an imagined offense; it had never happened. But a hand was raised just halfway at the oath to tell the truth, the whole truth and nothing but the truth.)

The New York Legislature amended the law in 1967 to allow divorce on the grounds of "mental cruelty", still a fault-based ground, but better because lawyers in cases without violence or conduct verging on the criminal, strung together a series of tepid allegations of "cruelty"; enough to pass muster before judges sick of being morality police.

(An aside: in the second year of my career, while I was with my first firm, Remington, Gifford, Wiley and Williams in Rochester, I took a divorce before a Supreme Court Justice at the Hall of Justice. The manner in which justices handled the testimony of default divorces varied widely. In this case, the Justice asked the plaintiff to come forward, take the oath and sit in the witness chair. He then asked the witness: "Are the allegations in your complaint true?" Answer: "Yes, Your Honor." Justice: "All right, divorce granted."

I never said one word.

As I walked back down the aisle heading for the door one of my colleagues whispered, with a smirk, "Nice job, John.")

It would be 2010 before New York law was finally changed again to allow so-called "no-fault divorce". Now the parties could merely cite "irreconcilable differences" as the grounds for divorce.

But, earlier, there was a second unfortunate feature of New York divorce: whichever spouse owned an asset kept that asset free and clear of any claim by the other spouse, as separate it wasn't so called "separate property", meaning property that the spouse *brought into* the marriage. Title was everything. So if, say, a dominant spouse saw to it that he owned all the assets, the departing wife would shuffle off into the sunset with a little cloud over her head, saying: "I lost everything."

Now, you can say what you like about "judicial activism", but there are times when without it justice is just a word. In the seminal New York *Majauskas* case the discussion probably went something like this (I like to romanticize it somewhat): "Judge, all the assets are titled to my client, and the law is that he keeps them." The Judge: "I know the law. *We're going to change it.*"

After this case, the New York Legislature codified the ruling, passing the so-called "EDL", or "Equitable Distribution Law". This meant that spouses needed to achieve a fair division of marital assets, including valuable pension rights.

I used to tell my clients that marital property was all property which the marriage surrounds.

Clients often expressed the worry that if, say, they moved out of the house, they'd lose everything as punishment. I used to tell them, "If the book of your marriage is 500 pages long, and if on page 499 it says you moved out to avoid more unpleasantness, that does not mean that the first 498 pages will be ignored by the court."

With key changes in the law New York came to recognize that a marriage is, among other things, *an economic partnership* and should be treated as such; and wisely, the final economic results should not turn on an assessment of fault.

There two exceptions: "wasteful dissipation of assets" (husband buys a Porsche, or claims to have lost all the marital assets at the racetrack), and "egregious conduct" (such awful conduct that it would be unjust to reward the actor with a fair division of assets. Almost like the common law doctrine of *clean hands*; one who seeks justice must not have sullied it with bad conduct).

Ineluctably, it wasn't long before I had the classic "egregious conduct" case.

I represented the wife. A good lawyer was on the other side, and we, and the clients, were working well toward a written settlement resolving the property and custody issues.

During the process, both spouses had connected with significant others, and things were progressing nicely..........

..........until my client and her boyfriend drove the daughter over to the husband's house for her weekend visitation.

The husband met them in the driveway with a shotgun, and with his daughter watching, *shot and killed my client's boyfriend in the driveway*.

Later, in the Judge's chambers, I asserted that the husband had committed egregious conduct of such a nature that all the marital assets should be awarded to my client. The court agreed, awarding title to all the marital assets. The husband wasn't going to need the assets in prison, which is where he was headed.

The case is an aberration; divorce cases are often characterized by hot air, but seldom by violence such as happened here.

I hasten to add that lawyers strive to achieve settlements of the issues, and express the same in written so-called "Settlement Agreements" or "Separation Agreements", which resolve all the financial issues, as well as custody and support issues.

I often told my clients that divorce can be civilized; that sometimes events overtake us; things we didn't want, didn't ask for and didn't expect. The important thing was for everyone to be able to move forward, to survive, to find life again. And I usually told my clients at our first conference, when dark skies cast a pall over everything, "You will see that there is Life After Divorce."

RICKY

Here, I depart from my use of pseudonyms for my clients, except for Ricky, the irrepressible adoptive child in the story. I use the pseudonyms "Sue" and "George" for the foster parents.

Sue and George had already adopted four young siblings when they received a call in the middle of the night. Social Services had a child, Ricky, just months old, whose leg had been broken by his mother.

Here, a word about the heroes in the child protective wing of the Ontario County Department of Social Services. When they learn of a child in danger, they swarm to his or her defense; they surround the child; they protect the child; and they often remove the child from the home where harm has occurred.

There's a tension here: in New York, the law protects children, but also promotes the natural family as the place where the child should be. So, while DSS has the authority to remove a child from a harmful environment, it is also charged with the duty to use its resources to re-unite the child with family where possible.

Sue and George received Ricky into their care as a foster child. Meanwhile, the biological mother received enough counseling to warrant his return into her home.

It was short-lived. When DSS discovered that Ricky had been burned upon his return to his mother, they began proceedings for the permanent termination of her parental rights.

This tedious process was all part of a *five-year* effort to sever the mother's parental rights and to advance Sue and George's petition for adoption. As is often the case with foster parents, they must suffer the frustrations inherent in the termination proceedings, the delays, the endless court appearances, the frequent updated reports, the home visits. And they need an attorney to stand with them, whose fees are not covered by the court system. Not until the child is actually placed for adoption does the state pay those fees; the legal costs in the runup are the sole responsibility of the foster parents.

In Ricky's case, his biological mother was convicted of the crime of injuring him; she appealed the conviction. Unsuccessfully, but time-consuming, like months.

Ultimately, the mother's parental rights were also terminated after a lengthy, multi court appearance hearing. She also appealed the termination, again unsuccessfully. Again, time-consuming.

In all of this, the foster parents are powerless observers. They must participate in most of the court appearances, but they have no ability to direct the outcome of the termination proceedings or the criminal proceedings, or the appeals. It's as though they are passengers on a slow moving bus.

Meanwhile, time marched on, and through it all, Sue and George were Ricky's safe harbor.

I was privileged to represent them, and watched Ricky grow into a delightful four, then five, year-old. Ruddy complexion, square face, open countenance; blond crew cut. And a keen wit and sense of humor.

On some occasions when I would call, Ricky would answer the phone. I would identify myself, and Ricky would call out: "It's John! We're going to court!"

Finally, adoption day. The caseworkers, bless them, showed up in force, bringing flowers, balloons, presents, their smiles celebrating the special day. The courtroom, a rainbow of festive colors.

I have seen judges cry at such occasions, knowing the child's journey and the wonder and joy that a forever home brings.

But no crying in this case, because when I looked around the courtroom for Ricky after the Order of Adoption was officially signed, I didn't see him. Sue said, "He's over there telling jokes to the judge." I asked Ricky, "What jokes?" He said, "Why is math so sad?" I said I didn't know. "Because it has so many problems!"

On his way home from court, Ricky asked Sue and George from the back seat of the car: "Now that I'm adopted, don't you think you should call me Richard?"

He's about eleven now, and thriving. He is a joy.

The words from an anonymous poem, "My Own Child", sum it up:

> And I will tell you apart from a thousand seeds grown wild
> And in my heart, I'll know that you are my own child

"HERE'S YOUR NEWBORN CHILD"

When my career began, adoptions could be carried out privately, without involvement by social agencies.

A fairly typical scenario would be a young woman at the dawn of her sexuality would become pregnant. Utterly unsuited for parenthood for one reason or for a constellation of reasons, she would be encouraged to surrender the child to adoptive parents.

Her doctor would connect with a childless couple seeking to adopt, who would in turn contact an attorney, who would prepare the necessary papers.

There were no requirements that the young mother have counseling; that she demonstrate that she fully understood the import of giving up the child; that she have an attorney; that a social agency would investigate the home of the putative parents; that after signing the papers there would be a waiting period for her to reconsider; that there would be no provision for her to receive updates about her child after the formal adoption; that the adoption was final.

On two occasions as a young lawyer, I actually picked up a newborn from the hospital and delivered the child to the home of waiting adoptive parents. It was permissible then.

Looking back now, it is inconceivable that this could have happened. But at the time it was not unusual. However, shortly after my first experiences with such adoptions, New York State passed much-needed laws requiring oversight of adoptions. No longer could well-meaning doctors and lawyers carry out an adoption without the involvement of social agencies, investigations, formal court appearances, reports to the court and other mechanisms to insure that the adoption was in the best interests of the child.

Caseworkers are the angels watching over endangered children, and they are part of the celebration when the final papers are signed.

"I'LL SUPPORT THE CHILD BECAUSE I'M A NICE GUY"

"Ok. Yes. I know. It is my child, and I fully intend to support it. But remember, I have my truck payment and my boat, not to mention my golf membership. I also help my girlfriend with her car payment. But anyway, I know my responsibility. What's the going rate now? Fifteen dollars?"

An exaggeration, but not by much.

When I started my practice, there was no standard for child support. Truly, the rate *was $15.00 per child*. It would stay at that level for awhile, and then without any discernable event, it would morph up to $20.00, then $25.00, $30.00 and so on. At the time of the big change it was at $50.00 per week.

What was "the big change?" The Child Support Standards Act, which set standards for support expressed as a percentage of the non-custodial parent's income, and required that support orders be in compliance except where the amount would be unjust or inappropriate.

Basic child support would be calculated at 17% of the combined parental income pro rated between the parents. For one child. 25% for two, 29% for three, 31% for four and 35% for more than four.

Income would such things as wages, dividends, capital gains, interest, deferred income, most government cash benefits such as unemployment and fringe benefits. Also, the *support magistrate* would be able to *impute* income based upon, among other things, a parent's *ability* to earn. So an intentional slacker could be ordered to pay child support in accordance with his true abilities.

Not only that, but in addition to the basic support amount, the non-custodial parent would be required to contribute to the costs associated with heath care, education and child care.

Joe could still be a nice guy, but now he would also be a financially responsible parent.

The girlfriend? Who knows? Maybe *her* child's father would pay child support to make up the slack.

WHEN TO FIRE A CLIENT

In matrimonial actions in Supreme Court such as divorce, and in Family Court, the issue of custody can be very difficult for all parties, for the court and for the attorneys. A number of issues must be resolved.

In many cases, the parties can work out a joint custody arrangement in writing for presentation to and approval by the court.

Such an agreement typically provides that the father and the mother will share responsibility and authority respecting the child or children.. The decision-making process will be shared on all matters having a significant impact on the child's life, including, but not limited to medical care, religious upbringing, school vacations and trips, summer camp and extra-curricular activities and associations.

The agreement states a goal of cooperation by the parties in raising the child.

Often, the so-called Child's Bill of Rights is set forth, typically reciting a series of tenets to insulate the child from the pressures sometimes generated by the parents. Here it is:

The Child's Bill of Rights

1. The right not to be asked to choose sides.
2. The right not to be told details of disputes between the parents.
3. The right not to be told "bad things" about the other parent's personality or character.
4. The right to privacy when talking to either parent on the telephone.
5. The right not to be cross-examined by one parent after spending time with the other.

6. The right not to be asked to be a messenger from one parent to the other.
7. The right not to be asked by one parent to tell untruths to the other.
8. The right not to be used as a confidant regarding disputes between the parents.
9. The right to express feelings, or to choose not to express feelings.
10. The right not to be made to feel guilty by either or both parents.

Finally, the agreement sets for the arrangements for physical residence, time-sharing, vacations, information-sharing and child support.

Most cases are resolved with such an agreement, not easily, but sensibly. The alternative to a *meeting of the minds* as expressed in a comprehensive and fair agreement is a *meeting in court* for a trial, which is certain to create or perpetuate a hostile environment, with the child in the middle.

Despite the advantages of such an agreement there are times when one or both parents cannot lay their bitterness aside, and child custody becomes a contest, a legal joust, which only hurts the child.

I probably worked with my client and opposing counsel on hundreds of settlement agreements, but one stands out.

My client counted the hours in the week and doggedly and unreasonably insisted that the child's physical residence be with him exactly, mathematically, half the time, and that he decide what activities the mother could, and could not, do with the child. No amount of discussion, counter-proposals or conciliatory gestures by the parties and counsel could mollify him. It was as tough the child was his *possession*.

Opposing counsel was making a strong case that the child was exhibiting signs of stress caused by the wrangling of the parents. Opposing counsel and I knew we were approaching the breaking point. It was clear to all that the child's best interests were not being served in the contentious atmosphere my client was creating.

Finally, in an office conference with me my client said his small child said to him: "Is today a Mommy day or a Daddy day?"

At that point, I knew I could not continue presenting my client's unreasonable demands to opposing counsel.

I told my client to consult with another attorney; I was withdrawing. Ethics rules limit the circumstances where an attorney, with court permission once a case has started, can terminate the attorney-client relationship; there are times when a court will not allow an attorney to withdraw. But where the attorney has a justifiable reason he can withdraw providing he gives reasonable notice and cooperates in the transfer of the file to another attorney. Among the instances where an attorney may withdraw from representing a client the situation where the client insists on a course of action with which the attorney has a fundamental disagreement and the disagreement cannot be reconciled.

Such was the case here.

I often told my clients: "To diminish the other parent in the eyes of the child is to diminish the child."

I don't regret the matrimonial practice, as difficult as it could sometimes be. It often took some time, but in most cases the parents did act in the best interests of the child, as difficult as it was to lay aside their grievances. Still, there were so many cases where one parent or the other, or both, seemed to relish conflict: the joy of petty victories; the agony of defeat. For some, going to Family Court was a virtual *hobby*. Lawyers earnestly try to diffuse the anger; sometimes it is not possible.

I found that most clients wanted to be able to tell their story, and being a listener was one of the roles played by an attorney, because it was important; it was the right way to help a client; and because the only alternative was telling the story in a courtroom.

THE BEST ANSWER EVER

Dad owned a machine shop, Acme Tool & Die, Inc. His two sons, Frank and Will, worked in the business, making it a family affair. It was a small, and struggling, business that had honorably survived on a shoestring for decades.

When Dad died, Will took over and both he and Frank continued, along with three or four employees, to run the business.

They did not own the building in which the business was conducted. They rented it from a man named Arnold.

Frank and Will's sister called me one day. There had been a fire in April of 2015, causing $160,000 damage. Arnold's insurance company paid that amount to Arnold, and, in turn, took his rights to pursue Frank, Will *and the corporation* in subrogation. In other words, the insurance company now possessed the legal right to sue for the $160,000 loss it suffered in paying the claim. The subrogation of Arnold's claim gave the insurance company a necessary interest to pursue damages.

The sister had been a client already. She said that her brothers needed an attorney, but the attorneys they had consulted all wanted hefty retainers, which they could not afford. They needed representation.

Could I help?

Yes, I told her; I had represented whole family through the years. When Will and Frank contacted me they told me up front they had no funds to pay legal fees. I told them I would represent them and we'd figure fees out later.

The insurance company had brought suit naming Frank, Will and the company itself as defendants, claiming, on one theory or another, that each was responsible for the loss.

The facts played out at an examination before trial brought on by the insurance company attorney. An EBT is a proceeding in a civil case where the parties' attorneys have an opportunity to examine opposing parties about the facts and damages in the case. It's a procedural mechanism to attempt to avoid a "trial by ambush".

At the EBT it was established that Will actually owned the business. His brother Frank was an *employee.*

One day after work Frank came back to the business property to burn some personal papers and other materials in a barrel on the business property, behind the building. It was after hours, and Will had gone home.

Arnold, the building owner, had told Frank and Will not to burn anything on the property. If they needed to, they should do it across the road, where there was a burn barrel. Despite this, Frank started the fire in the barrel behind the building, and then *returned home,* thinking the fire, down to embers, would just burn out.

Unfortunately, the embers set the grass on fire, and it traveled to the building.

By the time they came to me they were already in default in the lawsuit. They had not put in a formal Answer to the complaint, though Will had written the plaintiff's attorney to offer a payment plan. He did so in the hope he might arrange a feasible settlement plan, despite the fact that he was in no way responsible for the fire. His fear was that if by some chance a judgment against him were taken, he would be forced into bankruptcy, something he wanted to avoid.

I brought on a motion for an extension of their time to answer. Over the plaintiff's objection, the judge granted my motion, and I put in an answer. In it, we admitted Frank's wrongdoing and *consented to a judgment against him.* It's called *confession of judgment.* But we asserted that neither the company, Acme Tool & Die, Inc., nor Will had any liability whatsoever.

The attorney for the insurance company said his client would not withdraw the claim against Acme or Will. The reason: Frank already had a large IRS judgment against him, so the insurance company would never recover from him. As is customary in civil litigation, it would go after the parties with so-called *deep pockets*. In truth, neither Acme nor Will had deep pockets; they lacked funds with which to pay a judgment.

I could not dissuade the plaintiff's counsel to accept confession of judgment against Frank and dismiss the cause of action against Acme and Will.

So, we went to trial, both attorneys agreeing to waive a jury and try the case in front of the judge.

In the EBT Plaintiff's counsel had exhibited a penchant for endlessly asking questions about matters irrelevant to the issues at hand, and when he displayed that habit at trial I repeatedly objected. (The catch-all objection is "Your Honor, I object; it's irrelevant, incompetent and immaterial.") At one point when counsel asked about something extraneous to the facts at issue and I objected, the judge said to opposing counsel, "*What difference does it make?* Objection sustained."

Counsel called Frank as his first witness, and Frank very forthrightly took all the blame for the fire. He also acknowledged that *he had been told not to burn* where he did, and that he, and he alone, was responsible for negligently leaving the property before the fire was out. He made it clear the he would not oppose a judgment against himself for the $160,000. In fact, he asked for it.

Plodding onward in what I thought was a hopeless effort to pin liability on Acme and on Will, counsel called Will as his second witness.

After Will repeated that he wasn't present when the fire started, that *he had specifically told his brother not to use the barrell on the property*, and neither he nor his company had any responsibility for the fire, two things happened.

First, counsel asked one too many questions.

Second, Will gave the greatest answer any client of mine ever gave in any litigation. I knew it was coming.

Counsel: "So, if as you say the fire was caused only by your brother, did you fire him?"

Will: "No."

Counsel: "Why not?"

Will: "**Because he sits next to me at Thanksgiving.**"

It was over. I gripped my chair to avoid jumping up and down.

As we had requested, the judge threw out the cause of action against Acme and Will, and granted judgment against Frank.

I don't know whether that judgment is dischargeable in bankruptcy. I didn't handle such matters. But a quick look into it tells me that tax debts are treated differently than other kinds of debt when you file for bankruptcy. In most cases, taxes are not dischargeable though there are some exceptions such as fraud, mistakes or an undue hardship. Whether or not Frank can establish hardship I do not know, but I hope so.

His honesty was refreshing.

THE WORM TURNED. TWICE.

My good friend, John R. Kennedy, and I were trying a divorce case before Hon. James R. Harvey, Supreme Court Justice.

This was during the time when New York divorce laws required that a divorce be based upon *cruel and inhuman treatment* within a five year period prior to commencement of the action.

I represented the wife, who sought the divorce; John, the husband, who vigorously opposed it. That in itself was somewhat unusual, given the old lawyers adage that a marriage dead to one party is dead to both. (Forgive me, but the husband was immovably obtuse and rigid.)

In any event, while there were ugly exceptions, most proofs of cruel and inhuman treatment amounted to bruised feelings, unkind verbal insults or callous, but not violent, behavior. Such allegations, proofs, were usually sufficient to convince a bored justice to grant a divorce; and the real issues were usually "keeping your eye on the money". In other words, the divorce was quite often a given, and the court would be called upon to determine an *equitable distribution of marital property*.

But with John and I, the grounds for the divorce *were* the threshold issue.

My client was the plaintiff, and during the first day of trial we adduced a litany of alleged cruelty perpetrated by the husband. Most of the instances of cruelty were, as usual, dramatically exaggerated but provable.

I'll never forget this: at the end of the first day of trial, Judge Harvey waived his finger at John, and said, "You better settle this case, based on what I've heard today."

John was a good lawyer. And unflappable. So when I chuckled at him as we left the courtroom, he just smiled like a genial padre, hands folded piously in front.

During the second day of trial, John called his client, the husband, and together they countered all the allegations made by my client. If my client's testimony had been a trickle, John's client's was a flood.

And, so, at the end of the day Judge Harvey waggled his finger at *me*, and said, "After what I've heard today, the plaintiff's cause of action for divorce is *denied*!" Now, that's like a sentence: you are yoked to the person you've come to detest for life.

The worm had turned. It was the only time in my career that I lost a divorce case!

Remember; it was a trial on grounds, when you needed the weight of the credible evidence to persuade the court that the defendant was guilty of cruel and inhuman treatment. Denial of a divorce was unusual.

John was too much of a gentleman to gloat, but he gave me a look, like, *I told you so*. For years afterwards we laughed about the case. John laughed a little harder.

Lawyers know that, inevitably, there are days when you might better have stayed in bed.

There was a lesson here: *Never* count your chickens before they are hatched!

But there is a sequel: *the wormed turned again.*

Shortly after our trial, the New York State Legislature passed the so-called "No Fault Divorce Law", which required a mere showing of *"irreconcilable differences".* If just one of the two parties to the marriage claimed irreconcilable differences, there was no defense to it.

Since irreconcilable differences was a different ground from cruel and inhuman treatment, the first trial was not "law of the case"; was not a bar to a new action. We got the divorce on the new grounds, and proceeded to the tedious issue of how to untangle the couple's considerable assets.

Afterwards, John and I, each having been once battered, went golfing.

John is gone now, but I still see him walking his darn old brown dog when I drive by a field near his home. He was a lawyer's lawyer, honest, ethical, hardworking; a credit to the profession, and I miss him.

ADVANCE PLANNING

THE PERFECT WILL GONE WRONG

Niece Judy knew her Uncle Ed wasn't well. In fact, he was terminally ill. He lived alone in a cobblestone home on some 60 acres.

Niece Judy had an idea: she would invite Uncle Ed into her home. She would care for him.

But first, some business, right before the move.

She took Uncle Ed to a psychiatrist, a medical doctor and a lawyer in succession, all the consults calculated to produce The Perfect Will. With two stellar opinions as to Uncle Ed's mental and medical competence, and *the kindly ministrations of Niece Judy's own personal lawyer*, a fine document was prepared and executed with due formality.

Did I mention that according to the will Uncle Ed's entire estate would pass to his loving niece upon his demise?

There was just one minor problem. Uncle Ed felt that he had been had. Niece Judy's kindness masked an obvious ulterior motive; it was palpably enough to suggest to Uncle Ed that Niece Judy's affection was, let's say, disingenuous.

Uncle Ed's lifetime home was less than five miles from Zimmerman & Tyo's offices. He came into my office; we were mutual strangers, having never met. He related the facts to me, and said, "I want a new will."

We prepared it according to his instructions, which meant that his entire estate would pass to a cousin, not Niece Judy.

As predictably as a rising moon, Niece Judy initiated a will contest soon after Uncle Ed died. In probate, the burden is on the proponent to establish due and proper execution of the will with at least two witnesses, under the supervision of an attorney. Further, that the testator was upwards of 18 years of age, and in the opinions of the attesting witnesses, was of sound mind, memory and understanding and not under any restraint, and in all respects competent to make a Will. Finally, that the Testator could read, write and converse in the English language and did not appear to be suffering from any physical difficulties of sight, hearing or speech and impressed the witnesses as being a rational person.

I should mention that an attorney puts his or her personal imprimatur on every will; on every legal document he or she prepares, for that matter.

I should also mention that in fifty-five years, no will we ever prepared was knocked out, and that includes Uncle Ed's. The niece's will contest to declare the will invalid failed, and we administered the estate in accordance with Uncle Ed's wishes.

(An aside: a very nice lady client called me one day to cancel her appointment for a will. She said, "I've had some mental issues, and I'm in the hospital." I wished her well and asked her to call me when she was feeling better. She did, to re-schedule the appointment. I told her, "I don't want to offend you, but we should have a note from your doctor........" She understood completely, and provided the note. A failure to take that precaution would possibly fuel an attempt to contest the will by a disgruntled distributee. As I've told clients for decades: "This legal stuff might seem boring, but it can be quite thrilling some times.")

The Scottish poet Robert Burns's quote has application here: "The best laid plans of mice and men often go awry." So it was with the niece.

OLD WILLS NEVER DIE

I'll call it The Smith Will; it would fit nicely under The You Wanted To Be A Lawyer heading.

When someone comes in whose loved one has died, they need an attorney to negotiate Surrogate's Court. So, if there's a will, it's a *probate* matter, and once the will is accepted as legitimate by the Court, an executor/rix is appointed to carry out the wishes of the testator. If there's no will, it's an *administration*, and New York has rules as to who has priority in administering the estate, and, ultimately, inheriting it; a pecking order, so to speak.

To probate a will, you need a petition signed by the named executor/rix, a death certificate, the original will, affidavits of the persons who witnessed the will, and a listing of the persons, called *distributees*, who would benefit if there was no will. The rationale for identifying the distributees is this: if there was any hanky-panky, they would be the ones likely to know about it, and have an interest in telling the court about it. So, for example, a lady has three daughters; the will leaves the entire estate to two of them. All three need to be notified of the existence of the will. The daughter not named in the will can sign a so-called *waiver*, by which she would basically sign off from any interest she might have in the estate; or she could refuse to sign the waiver, in which case she would receive a citation issued by the Court to appear to state her objection to the will; or she could flat-out contest the will.

These rules do not mean that we put a will to a *vote*; they simply insure that a person's next of kin are aware of the existence of a will and that they have an opportunity to be heard in situations where they would raise a *legitimate* objection to it.

As a practical matter it is extremely difficult to contest a will; a successful will contest is rare. One has to show a basis on which the will should not be *admitted to probate*: undue influence, fraud, forgery, improper execution, lack of mental capacity, intoxication, duress, the will is incomplete, the witness statements are missing or inadequate, another, competing will, etc.

The procedures in Surrogates Court are intended to negate any or all of such objections, so that when a will is probated it is above reproach.

Though as I have mentioned, no will we ever prepared was denied probate; there were two unsuccessful challenges.

We prepared Walt Smith's will in 2020. When Walt died in 2022, his son came to us for assistance in probating it. We submitted all the necessary documents for a routine probate.

But, wait! The Court Clerk e-mailed me: there was a previous will. Now, that would not be unusual: people often revisit their wills to update them or add something or change something.

But when the new wills are prepared, we shred the old ones! The Court never knows about the old will, *nor does it need to*. The new will expressly *revokes* any previous ones.

But in the Smith case, someone, for some reason, had *filed* the old will in Surrogate's Court twelve years earlier! This was a first, coming at about the fifty-third year of my career. There was no attempt to probate the earlier will; indeed, Walt was still *alive*. We never knew *why* the old will was filed. Such a filing was rare. Let's say a lawyer prepares a will for a client, who executes it. The lawyer and client agree on who is keeping the original, usually the lawyer, and the client gets a copy. When the client walks out the door, *why would the lawyer file it?* The client is still living and can change the will at any time.

It's possible someone filed it for safekeeping. But no lawyer would ordinarily do it because there is no point to it, no need to file it. And all wills state that the testator "does make, publish and declare this to be my last will and testament, *hereby revoking all wills and codicils heretofore made by me.*

But in the Smith case, the New York rule is: since the will was *filed*, even if not *offered for probate,* the Court is *on notice* of it, and the persons named in that earlier will have an *interest which is possibly adversely affected* by the new will.

This is a nutty rule.

But in the Smith case the Court, following the New York rule, required that we notify all the persons who would have received an interest under the old will. And there were *eight* such persons, living all over the US of A. This meant we had to find those persons, and explain all of this, and ask that they sign a waiver to indicate that they consented to the new will. (We don't *need* them to consent; if they don't we will obtain a citation requiring that they come into court to tell the judge what their objection is, and it needs to be a legitimate objection. It just makes the proceedings far more tedious.) Seven of the eight signed and returned the waivers.

We had to get a court date, prepare a citation for the eighth person to appear in court, and have it served. In Texas. (Find her, get an address, find a process server, have it served, pay the process server's fees; and did I mention, do it all before the next court date set by the judge?) After all that, she signed and returned the waiver so the court appearance was not necessary. She couldn't have done that at the beginning? Everyone else did.

That it was necessary to locate all the legatees from the first will was frustrating, because Walt had just *one beneficiary: his son*, who inherited the entire estate. The need to locate all of the previously mentioned legatees, prepare and send waivers, track their return, file them and then obtain a citation for a court appearance for the eighth legatee all served to delay the probate and add to the legal fees for our client.

To this day, the rule requiring notice to the persons mentioned in the earlier will is a head-scratcher, and just one of the many reasons a lawyer gets grouchy.

CLARA

For eighteen years, my office was on Main Street, Shortsville, in a two-story residence which is now our home. My office was what is now our dining room. The position of my desk afforded me a narrow view of Main Street, including the sidewalk, where passersby would catch my eye.

One such passerby was the retired Redjacket Latin teacher, Clara. On the occasions when I was outside, she and I would strike up a conversation. One day, she told me of her concern that she would develop dementia, just like her mother. She asked me if I would be willing to serve as her power of attorney, and, ultimately, as her executor, adding that I would know when the time came that I would be needed. I agreed to do it, and the papers were executed.

I hasten to add that in my five decades of practice there were no more than six or seven clients for whom I agreed to act as so-called *attorney-in-fact* (power of attorney). I always advised clients that wherever possible they should name a loved one or friend to serve in that capacity.

Every couple of years, Clara would ask me to come to her home, where she showed me all her papers. And she expressed the fervent desire that she be able to remain in her home if she became unable to attend to her affairs.

She was right: when the time came ten or fifteen years later, we knew it.

To provide for her care, Liz and I gathered together a team of seven women, none of whom were professional nurses, to provide round-the-clock care for her. Truly, it was like running a business, because, unlike many household in the affluent urban areas where "nannies" were employed without any wage reporting or benefits, Liz and I followed all the rules: federal and state withholding, Workers Comp, New York State Disability, federal and state and unemployment. Only a fool dukes it out with the government.

We did provide for Clara in her own home, just as she had wished.

Now, at the times when Clara had shown me her papers and assets, she told me that she owned *three hundred acres in the Napa-Sonoma valley in California*. On the property was a two-acre ranch, rented out to a couple who pestered her to buy it; they were overbearing about it. They were renting it for the paltry sum of *$150 per month!* Clara had told me that the place needed some upgrading, but the rent she was collecting was unreasonably low.

Knowing that, Liz and I made a trip to Vacaville, California. There, we contacted a contractor, and $15,000 (peanuts now, but not then) later the ranch house was much improved. Having asked the renters to vacate the property so the renovation could proceed, we re-rented it to new tenants on completion for $900 per month, a manageable and reasonable rent for the place.

When Clara passed away we probated her will in New York, and contacted a California attorney to do the same there so that title could transfer out of the estate. The will left the Napa-Sonoma property to a cousin.

Looking back now it is humbling knowing that Clara placed her trust in us, and that with the help of local community members we were able to honor her wishes.

GIFTS FROM THE HEART

Clara was generous, leaving most of her estate to charities. Instances of charitable giving were fairly numerous with clients who lacked close family. Two come to mind.

Paul Bailey and his wife, Mary, lived alone in the Village of Shortsville. They had no children. Age was taking its toll on both of them, Mary, more than Paul. They watched over, took care of, each other.

One day, Mary could not get out of the bathtub. Paul called 911, which dispatched the volunteer ambulance of Citizens Hose Company.

The ambulance crew gave assistance to Mary, helping her out of the tub, safe and sound.

Paul never forgot it, then, or after Mary passed away.

Years later, he told me he wanted to leave his estate to Citizens Hose Company to help it buy an ambulance.

When Paul died, his estate left *$80,000* to Citizens Hose Company; enough to purchase a brand new ambulance.

Before his death, Paul needed some assistance paying his bills and, in general, sorting through his general affairs. He asked if I would serve as his attorney-in-fact, or power of attorney.

I knew his situation and, as mentioned, it was one of the few times in my career that I would so act.

For several years, he would call the office and speak to my wife, Liz, who was our bookkeeper, and who kept track of Paul's money. "It's Bailey! And I need fifty bucks!" he would say. Liz would go to the bank and cash a check for $50 for him.

With the $50, Paul would go to the florist and buy flowers for the ladies who cared for him at Ressie Jone's adult home.

Country lawyer? Where else would you feel a heartbeat like that?

Or a thrill like the one I had the day I went to the bank with Paul. When we left the bank he suggested I ride with him back to the office. Just one block, but I didn't to offend him. At 15 mph, it was one of the most hair raising rides of my life.

Another client was Floyd "Toad" Gilman, as he was nicknamed.

He was a member of the Manchester Fire Department for decades. He lived in one house his entire life, where he and his sister were raised by their parents. When they died in their time, one after the other, he remained in the house. He never married and had no children or relatives.

When we prepared his will, he wanted his entire estate to pass to the Village of Manchester for its fire department.

That is what happened, and the amount he left was enough to jump start the construction of a brand new fire hall and village office.

There's a plaque on the wall of the fire hall commemorating the gift.

The plaque bears an engraved image of Toad. He's in his fire department dress blues and uniform hat.

He looks proud.

"NO! I WON'T GO!"

Bill and Ann have been married for over fifty years. Ann was a lovely and accomplished lady, with an important presence in the community.

The couple had come in for wills, health care proxies and powers of attorney, all of which were prepared and they executed.

Years later, Ann got Alzheimer's Disease.

Bill cares for her at home, with some outside assistance. But, as is characteristic of the disease, as Ann's condition worsened, she became aggressive and angry, to the point that she experienced violent outbursts.

On one such occasion, Bill called 911, and an ambulance arrived. Bill explained the problem, and told the ambulance crew, "I have Ann's health care proxy."

Then he added: "She needs to go to the hospital."

But upon hearing that, Ann said, "No! I won't go to the hospital."

At that the ambulance personnel said, "We cannot take her to the hospital if she refuses to go."

Were they right?

Yes. The New York Health Care Proxy has effect *only if you are unable to make your own decisions*. It does not allow a provider to substitute his or her own judgment as to whether a decision is, or is not, a wise one made by a competent person.

So, to take an extreme case, suppose one is lying in a hospital bed unable to move, except for one finger. The doctor says, "We'd like to do an MRI today. Would that be ok?" The patient is not able to respond verbally. The doctor says if you would NOT want us to do that test, would you raise one finger?

If the patient does raise that finger, the medical personnel are bound by the patient's decision.

The bottom line: the New York Health Care Proxy is a good document that everyone should have. It typically comes into play in end-of-life decisions, where the giver of the proxy has told the agent that he or she does not want heroic efforts expended to extend a life where its quality is poor or non-existent. In other words, as most clients put it, "Pull the plug."

If Ann does go to the hospital, and if she becomes unable to express herself, *then* her husband Bill can use his best judgment under the circumstances when it comes time to make decisions.

End of life issues are difficult. A country lawyer sees them frequently, and feels it when they pass through his office. Who could not?

REAL ESTATE

HOUSEWARMING GIFTS TO MEGA INSURANCE COMPANIES

I preface my unkind remarks about title insurance companies with the fact that I was and am an advocate for the ordinary folks who sell or buy their homes, the places where they raise their families.

A young couple, Jim and Sally, want to buy their first home. Their offer is accepted. It is contingent on their ability to obtain mortgage funding.

Their application for a mortgage is successful; their lender issues a so-called *commitment letter*, which sets forth certain requirements, including clear title, which is established by seller's abstract of title, proposed deed, tax searches and a survey. Those documents were always sufficient until lenders began requiring *title insurance*.

When I started practicing law in 1967, we would obtain title insurance only in situations where there was a title issue, not easily solved. So, for example, a missing heir in the chain of title, which can fan out like the delta of a river, involving literally dozens of putative owners. Or an undischarged ancient mortgage. Or an old and abandoned railroad bed along the edge of the property. Or an old and deficient legal description. Or an easement or mortgage held by a now defunct entity. Or lakefront property, where one foot can be World War III.

Curing any of these problems could possibly require a lawsuit to quiet title, and that would not be feasible, considering the time constraints set out in the commitment letter, or, at a minimum, time-consuming investigation and research for curatives, not to mention the expense.

So, such a title could possibly involve *risk*.

A title insurance company would usually agree to insure the title for a fee. The title company would undertake the unlikely risk that some one or something from the past would show up and make demands on the title in exchange for a premium. In the transaction, there was *value for value*: that is, the title company got the premium and the would-be homeowner cleared the title.

But after the collapse of the savings and loan banks (see below), lenders began to require title insurance on every transaction. And the title insurance companies insisted on *perfect titles* or they would not insure them. Sellers' attorneys were expected to cure any and all title defects prior to closing. That included minor problems such as fences not on the true boundary line, driveway encroachments, common driveways, a neighbor's eaves over the line by inches, old oil and gas leases, minor deviations in names in the back title, etc.

Over the years, my paralegals and I spent literally thousands of hours on *title curatives*, so that at the closing our seller clients presented *perfect titles*.

At the closing on, say, a $150,000 mortgage loan our young buyers Jim and Sally, will have to pay for title insurance. The cost is usually between 0.5% and 0.7% of the loan amount. So, if Jim and Sally borrow $150,000, they will have to pay a big title insurance company something in the range of $750 to $1,050.

In reality, that is Jim and Sally's *gift* to the title insurance company, which has demanded and received a perfect title. If there are no unresolved title issues, then there are *no risks* in insuring the title.

I've referred to young buyers for dramatic effect, but the scheme of title insurance applies to everybody.

And here's the kicker: the premium paid by the kids buying their first home pays for a *mortgagee* title insurance policy that covers *only the lender*, not the home buyers. If they want to insure their so-called *fee title interest*, there's an additional premium.

I can honestly say that in my fifty-five year career no title insurance company ever lost *one penny* in the countless thousands of transactions I handled for my clients.

According to the American Land Title Association, title companies pay out losses on only about 7% of the premiums they collect.

A pretty good business model. But not for my clients.

Though I have railed about this for decades, the requirement of title insurance is so entrenched that it has become a given feature of all real estate transactions.

But wait! On March 7, 2024, after the above was written, President Joe Biden gave his State of the Union Speech to Congress. In it, among other issues of which he spoke, he said his administration is going to *eliminate the requirement of title insurance in federally backed mortgage loans*; he suggested it would save many home buyers "a thousand dollars".

I never thought I would hear that.

Of course, I am worried about the insurance companies, but I'm sure they'll find other things to insure, like broken golf clubs or something.

- FORECLOSURE: HAVE A GROUP HUG, SING KUBAYA AND GIVE HIM A DEED -

David and Valerie Smith owned a very modest home in Irondequoit. It became difficult to manage the home, as is often the case as people age.

So in November of 2008 they conveyed their home to a man I'll call Santiago, for $64,000. They took back a mortgage *for the entire purchase price* and set the interest rate at 4% at a time when the rates were at least double that. The mortgage required Santiago to make payments in monthly installments of Three Hundred Five and 55/100 Dollars for principal and interest until said Note and Mortgage, if not sooner paid, was paid in full on or about November 1, 2038. In addition to the requirement of monthly payments of principal and interest, the Note and Mortgage required Santiago to insure the mortgaged premises against fire and other risks, and to pay all taxes, assessments, sewer rents or water rates within thirty days after they are due.

All standard terms of a mortgage.

David Smith died in December of 2015.

Valerie Smith died in January of 2018.

When David Smith died, though, Santiago stopped making mortgage payments. Not only that, *he stopped paying the real property taxes*, and, as is customary in such cases the County of Monroe issued a Tax Lien Assignment to an investor; in this case, to Tower DBW II Trust 2012-2, by the terms of which its tax lien on the mortgaged premises for the year 2017 was sold. This would give Tower the right to command a deed to the property after the last day the taxes could be paid.

But in 2018 after Valerie's death without a will, we had gotten David and Valerie's sons, Charles and Allen, appointed by Monroe County Surrogate's Court as the Administrators of her estate. This would give them authority to take some kind of action regarding Santiago's delinquencies.

The first thing they did was pay all the back taxes, and then ask that I write a letter to Santiago, which I did. It was ignored.

Santiago then filed bankruptcy. Forgive me, I understand the purpose of bankruptcy, to eliminate debtors prisons, but it creates an automatic stay of all proceedings, including mortgage foreclosures, regardless of its outcome. No matter the ultimate outcome, it's a dodge, because it stays all creditor actions.

So, we had to wait until the bankruptcy was concluded before we could proceed to enforce the mortgage or pursue the alternative.

So began the odyssey called....... "foreclosure".

Complying with new rules intended to protect homeowners from predatory lenders and scams by those pretending to save homeowners from foreclosures, we initiated a foreclosure action by the service of a summons and complaint. Finding Santiago was never easy, but our process server found him at his place of employment.

At the initial court appearance in the Hall of Justice in Rochester, Santiago failed to appear. The court noted his absence and indicated that it would set another date (where, presumably, in the case of a pure default, I could submit a proposed judgment of foreclosure). But as I began to leave the courtroom, I heard, "Your Honor, we represent the defendant."

I had heard from nobody prior to the court appearance; not the defendant; nor any lawyer representing him.

The lawyer who spoke represented an organization whose function was to protect homeowners from foreclosure. But to my knowledge his appearance was spontaneous and unbidden. He had not connected with Santiago, but claimed to represent him. I don't know if the organization routinely appeared in default foreclosure proceedings, but it seemed so to me.

Somehow, this offended my sense of fairness, not to mention that the ethics I learned required that a lawyer actually have a relationship with a client to claim representation. Even a $1.00 retainer would suffice. I sense that if I did it, it would make The Wall Street Journal.

The court had no choice but to regard the attorney as the attorney of record, and an adjournment date was set. The lawyer would try to contact Santiago.

Along the way, a NYS required "mandatory settlement conference" date was set. Santiago himself never appeared and no acceptable offer was made by his attorney.

After several court appearances and long delays, we succeeded in obtaining a judgment of foreclosure.

Meanwhile, my clients were paying all the taxes and insurance on the property.

Meanwhile, gallingly, Santiago remained in the house, living large, refusing to pay for anything.

The judgment of foreclosure would allow my clients to pursue taking possession of the property. But Santiago wasn't moving. He was staying, rent free.

Ok, we would evict him.

But then, Covid hit. All the courts were effectively shut down. I do not remember the length of the delay, but it was considerable.

Eventually, we succeeded in selling the house for a high bid of just $35,000 at a foreclosure sale. The investor/buyer said he would get Santiago out.

Did I mention that I hugged him?

It had been some twenty-five months from commencement of the foreclosure action to the sale.

After the payment of closing costs, back taxes and legal fees, my clients netted just over $10,000. It wasn't much, but the clients were glad to have it over with.

In retrospect, although it sounds a little whiney, it seemed as though the defaulting homeowner turned squatter had all the rights, while my clients had none. They were patient and appreciative of our efforts, and understood completely when I joking told them if they ever found themselves in another foreclosure to *have a group hug, sing Kumbaya and give the defendant a deed to the property.*

HOW TO KEEP THE FAMILY CAMP IN THE FAMILY; OR NOT

Ever so often, clients would come in to discuss the family camp in the Adirondacks. It seems that half of Shortsville/Manchester had a cabin on Uncas Road near Inlet, New York. (An aside: during a stretch of each of three years, Liz and I drove to Inlet Town Court to represent a client's son or daughter in town court for a minor transgression. We always looked forward to an overnight in Inlet.) Anyway, the usual discussion centered around the clients wanting to keep the family camp in the family, in perpetuity. Understandably, the campground was a special place for the gathering of family and friends on weekends and vacations; a respite from the work week.

Often, the clients wanted to form a corporation and convey the title to the camp to the corporation.

Though the clients' desire that future family be able to experience the same wonderful times as they had was laudable, I was always successful in talking them out of forming a corporation; or, in fact, conveying the property to any other sort of entity.

The reasons were many.

How many shares of corporate stock would issue? What would be the price? Who, after the current owners, would do the bookkeeping, pay expenses? Would he or she be compensated? What would the shareholders' annual contribution to expenses be? What about inactive shareholders? After a generation or two, how many outstanding shares would there be? How, if at all, would they be redeemed? Who would get to actually use the property? How would priorities of usage be determined? Who would tend to maintenance and repair? Who would be the active managers, and how would they be selected? Would they be compensated? What would happen, forgive me, but, aside from a family feud, when capital repairs, like a new roof, were needed? Could the place be rented? Who would manage the rentals and account for the same?

In my 2018 Memoir, I speak of "the loveable mundane"; this is it. But to our clients, their heartfelt and well-intentioned hopes for their campsite were a genuine concern.

As gently as possible, I suggested that entity ownership would not be viable. I advised them to enjoy the camp and let future economic circumstances decide the future. Likely, one or more families with active interest would band together and purchase the property.

To my knowledge, Uncas Road is still Shortsville/Manchester North.

YOU BETTER GO GET A GOOD LAWYER

On two occasions I was privileged to represent clients in multi-million dollar purchases.

The first was acquisition of an ongoing electronics design and manufacturing business. Because of confidentiality I cannot divulge the name of the business, the purchase price or other details of the transaction.

But when the client brought the contract in and I saw the purchase price, I recall saying, in words or effect, "You better get a Rochester lawyer who handles big transactions." The client said, "No, I want you to handle it. The principles are the same; it's just that the numbers are bigger."

The financing of this transaction involved six or seven lenders. Representing the buyer, I was the hub of communications, and I remember having 60 e-mails the day before the closing.

It was a singular honor to represent my client, truly a Captain of Industry, in this transaction.

The second major, major transaction was the purchase of a large farm by longstanding clients of ours. I recall examining the real estate titles to the twenty-one parcels inherent in the transaction.

Representing this farm family in this transaction and through the years was, again, an honor.

Both of these clients are redolent of the Great American Spirit of entrepreneurship, knowledge, hard work, ethics, dedication, courtesy and respect for others.

It doesn't get any better than this for a country lawyer; or for any lawyer for that matter.

THE SIX BY TWELVE DRIVEWAY

It seems we used to get a lot of snow in upstate New York; not so much in recent years, (no matter what climate deniers think). One year a neighbor walked over to our house as I was shoveling the driveway, and complained that his neighbor to the west was throwing snow onto his property as he shoveled his driveway.

"Where is he putting it?" I asked.

"On my lawn."

"Is it in your way in any way? Is he throwing it on your driveway?"

"No. My driveway is on the other side. He's throwing it on my lawn."

This same neighbor used to complain that my secretaries parked their cars on the public street in front of his house (not blocking anything).

I said something like, "You know, if it's no harm to you, such as it would be if he were putting it in your own driveway, you just need to try to be a good neighbor." (I guess I spoke to him as I would a small child.)

My suggestion was met with steely resistence, and I returned to The Joy Of Shovelng.

When spring came, I noticed some paving equipment on the complaining neighbor's property, adjacent to the snow thrower's driveway.

He had the paving company install a driveway about twelve feet long and six feet wide right next to the snow-shoveling neighbor's driveway. It had no purpose whatsoever.

Now he could claim the neighbor was shoveling his snow onto his driveway!

In all the years since, I have never seen any use of the added driveway, even for parking a car.

The driveway is still there.

The offending neighbor is long gone.

YOU CAN'T MAKE THIS STUFF UP

A smattering of issues in real estate transactions:

Your client calls after the closing: "When we went to the house after the closing, we discovered that the sellers *took all the* **light bulbs**."

At the closing where you represent the buyers, the seller says: "We want to take the **totem pole** after the closing."

Your examination of the abstract of title and survey on a residential transaction reveals that there's a **Native American burial ground** on part of the property. (Until 2023 New York State was one of only four states with no protection for unmarked Native America burial sites. But in 2023 New York State passed the Unmarked Burial Site Protection Act, which requires that the finding of remains and/or artifacts be reported to the county medical examiner. The sale, destruction or removal of such items is now a Class E felony.)

At the closing, the lender's attorney says: "We can't close." You ask "Why not?" The attorney says: "The commitment letter requires a credit report to the day of closing. Your client's report, which we received this morning, shows a *new charge*." You check with your client; then respond: "He bought a $500 ring for his wife for a birthday present." Lender's attorney: "We can't close. We'll have to run it by the lender." I told my clients we would re-schedule the closing when we would show proof of their ability to afford the ring payments without forcing the lender into bankruptcy. (People in the elevator we rode on the way back from the closing to street level wondered at my mumbling.)

A sampling of the kinds of *physical* problems that routinely come to light in closings, aside from the *title* defects that show up in abstracts:

- the neighbor's fence is over the line, or vice versa
- the neighbor's tree hangs over our property, or vice versa
- the neighbor's eves hang over onto our property, or vice versa
- part of the neighbor's driveway "encroaches" onto my property, or vice versa
- our fence, or the neighbor's, is not on the survey line
- there are remnants of an old fence not on the property line
- there are remnants of a small concrete wall straddling the line
- the neighbor's clothes line crosses the back corner of our property
- the 20 year old immovable shed on our property is too close to the line
- the sellers have failed to remove junk or hazardous materials prior to closing
- the "broom clean" provision of the contract is breached; the place is filthy

Somehow, some way, these issues have to be resolved.

This is one of the ways migraines start.

THERE'S A DIVINITY THAT SHAPES OUR ENDS

True, I hadn't met Shakespeare yet when I was twelve years old.

But I knew "divinity".

Our neighborhood posse, that is, my South Wedge friends, Gerbers, as we called him, and Doug and Jimmy, used to walk over to Colgate Rochester Divinity School because they had a bowling alley in the basement, and they let us use it. And it was free!

Two lanes, no pin setter. We had to set our own pins. What fun. We were sort of like Urban Huckleberry Finns.

(I'd like to think that wonderful man, Reverend Hoagland, of The First Baptist Church I attended on South Avenue would be happy I was involved with divinity. I can still see his towering figure and imagine his avuncular, kindly sermons.)

In any event, now, looking backwards, I see something about shaped ends, because about three years after my graduation from law school, Colgate Rochester Divinity School merged with Crozer Theological Seminary from Upland, Pennsylvania. Several of the Crozer faculty relocated to Rochester. Remington, Gifford represented CRDS, and I wound up representing the incoming faculty members when they purchased homes in the area. Somehow one of the paths in my life led me back to the divinity school.

Here again, in this instance I wasn't yet a "country lawyer", but isn't there a link? Here I am fifty-four years later, looking back through the eyes of a country lawyer, seeing life experiences so warm they could be set in a meadow somewhere.

A FINAL WORD ABOUT REAL ESTATE

There is no aspect of a law office today that is more tedious, vexing and frustrating than real estate, as boring as it might be thought of.

If we look back to the 1970s, real estate was relatively straightforward, easily manageable and enjoyable. A deed, a mortgage; done, and we dealt face to face with local lenders.

But in the 1980s the savings and loans collapsed. As Investopedia puts it, it was "a slow-moving financial disaster." As an attorney in a rural area, I was not invited into the boardrooms of the banking industry, so my take on what happened is second-hand.

It's my understanding that among the reasons for the failure some one-third of the savings and loan institutions were that they were loaded with low-interest loans, coupled with unwise, sometimes fraudulent and speculative loans. The Federal Savings and Loan Insurance Corporation became insolvent, and -- surprise -- the taxpayers were saddled with a bailout.

My office, my paralegals and my clients, and those of every other law office, were left to deal with the aftermath of the crisis. The direct consequence of the collapse was -- another surprise -- *regulation*. And every law office in the country saw their real estate transactions take on formality that had theretofore not existed. Real estate closings now feature the assembly of a dizzying array of pre-closing requirements and documents culminating in an explosion of paperwork at a closing. In addition to the basic documents (abstract, tax searches, proposed deed, proposed mortgage) title insurance, surveys and endless and redundant disclosures and affidavits are required. If you've had a closing in the last twenty years, you know what I'm saying.

The players in a current real estate closing are numerous: buyer, seller, seller realtor, buyer realtor, seller attorney, buyer attorney, lender, lender attorney, abstract company, title insurance company, home inspector, loan officer, tax collector, insurance agent, credit reporter, employer, surveyor, existing mortgage-holder and others. The many pieces of the puzzle leading to closing cannot be ordered from providers all at once. They are assembled *ad seriatim*; for example, you can't order a survey without first obtaining an abstract redate; you can't order title insurance without the survey, and so on.

All must be coordinated to prepare for The Big Event, namely, the on-time closing on a date legislated by the lender.

A factor that distinguishes real estate from many other legal matters is that all the title issues, required disclosure notices, closing statements, agreed figures, mortgage discharges and buyers' down payment checks must be complete before the expiration of the lender's commitment letter. It's a scramble, and even if the attorneys for the buyers and sellers are ready, they often do not receive closing figures from the lender's attorney until literally hours before the closing.

In short: real estate is immediate, demanding and intense.

Inch by inch, the title companies will take over real estate, and has happened in many states, and the lawyers can go fish.

JUDGES

HOW TO MAKE A JUDGE ANGRY

We have seen a little about The Joy of Foreclosures.

They are incubators for headaches.

Early in my career, I was happily at work in my office when I received an urgent phone call from clients whom I'll call Henry and Sally Crandall.

They explained that they were "being foreclosed on."

When they came in, I learned that:

- indeed, they were in default in their mortgage payments;
- an action for forclosure had been started;
- they had been served with the summons and complaint;
- *and their time to appear in the action expired in two days*

It was Defcon Three.

I had no time to research anything, to review whatever mortgage documents they had, to run figures to try to gain an idea of how far they were behind, to call opposing counsel to try to work something out. But I knew that when time expires to answer a complaint you are at risk of a default judgment.

Now, I don't care who the lawyer is, but if he or she has any of the milk of human kindness, he or she is going to put in an appearance in this kind of situation.

It would be a stopgap, something to give some kind of protection to the clients; a breather, to try to figure out how to help them; to explore whether there is a way to save the home, in this case. Or, if not, to make other necessary arrangements.

In legal actions, what customarily follows service of a Summons and Complaint is an Answer. And that's what I breathlessly drafted on the spot and had the clients sign.

There are two kinds of Answers. One is to identify and assert every kind of *affirmative defense* the lawyer can think of, such as lack of standing, lack of possession of the original loan documents, defective notices of foreclosure, defective default notices, violation of the statute of limitations, lack of good faith negotiations, robosigning of critical documents, etc.

The other kind is a so-called "general denial" answer. With that kind of answer, you are generally denying all the claims in the complaint, without going line by line and admitting or denying each statement. Lawyers toss this kind of answer off like used Kleenex.

And that is the kind of answer I put in for the Crandalls.

I went back to work and forgot about the case, figuring I would hear from counsel for the plaintiff. And at that time we might be able to craft a settlement.

The clients were protected. *I didn't have a clue that I wasn't.*

Fast forward a few months when I received a call from the clerk of the Supreme Court Justice assigned to the case. He said, "The judge wants you up here in his chambers on the Crandall case *now*."

It didn't sound like an invitation to tea and crumpets, whatever they are.

It also didn't sound warm and encouraging; but it also didn't sound like I could ignore it. It didn't sound like something I might enjoy.

It sounded like my day was going to be memorable, and not in a good way.

Abandoning whatever I was working on at the time, I jumped in my car and headed through The Can of Worms, as the jumble of four-lanes leading to Rochester was called at the time.

After a curt greeting, the judge, whose name I have long and mercifully forgotten, but whose saturnine face and look of disdain I will not forget, initiated the following colloquy.

"Counsel, did you file the Answer in this case?"

"Yes, Your honor."

" In the Answer, you are denying all the allegations of the complaint?"

"Yes, Your Honor."

"Are your clients denying that they gave the mortgage?"

"No, Your Honor."

"Are they denying that they have defaulted in making all the payments?"

"No, Your Honor."

"WELL THEN, COUNSEL, HOW CAN YOU ENTER AN ANSWER THAT DENIES THAT THEY GAVE THE MORTGAGE OR FAILED TO MAKE ALL THE PAYMENTS?"

Now here, as I recall, I sheepishly said something like.....

"Your Honor, the came in at the last day and I was just trying..."

"But you had them sign a verification! That means they swear to the truth of their denial!"

"Um, yes, Your Honor."

Did I mention that I was a rookie lawyer at the time? That I looked thirteen years old?

Did I mention that I was aware that in New York State practice under the Civil Practice Law and Rules I needed to respond to the plaintiff's verified complaint with my clients' verified answer, but using a general denial answer was insupportable? My verified answer might have stated that my clients admitted the mortgage and the default, but.... insert some excuse for the default and pray for time to cure it; something like that.

Did I mention that in my fervor to protect my clients I did not have, or take, the time to research a general denial?

I felt like I should say something like, *"Your Honor, should I head over to the jail now, or wait for the police to pick me up?"* I suppressed the thought of defending myself by asking the Judge, "Your Honor, *weren't you a lawyer once*, before you were a judge? And didn't you try to help your clients?" Somehow, in the microsecond the thought crossed my mind, it occurred to me that His Honor would not have received my question with a warm smile. It is possible that a stout counterattack is a good defense, but not with a sitting Supreme Court Justice. And not when you are still wet behind the ears, whatever that means.

Was that little throb in my head just a headache, or was it a stroke?

A fleeting thought crossed my mind: Jimmy Swaggart in tears delivering his "I have sinned speech."

But after a terrifying silence, His Honor, with a thin smile I'm sure he felt was hilarity, said I could submit an amended answer.

My emotion severely contained, My Inner Self thought I had won the Lottery.

It's been so long that I do not have the faintest recollection of whether the Crandalls were able to save their home, but I do remember My Time With The Judge as if it were yesterday.

The judge was absolutely right, and for the remainder of my career I took care in knowing what could, and could not, legitimately be denied in a sworn legal document. It was a very valuable lesson.

And because of it, I do not remember ever going to jail. (Well, except for one night when I was an Assistant DA riding with a deputy sheriff. We were overtaken by a snow storm, and I spent a night in a cell.)

AN EARLY LESSON

I learned another valuable lesson in my very first year. Now, technically, I was not a country lawyer then, but it was something every lawyer, even those in flannel shirts living in the vicinity of cows would need to know.

It was 1967 and my first position as an attorney was with the Rochester firm, Remington, Gifford, Wiley and Williams. Five seasoned and respected attorneys on the 12th Floor of the Lincoln First Building. They displayed uncommon civility in all things The values I learned there have lasted all these years. I became the sixth lawyer with the firm, and it was a blessed start for a young lawyer, because the partners' standards and ethics were peerlessly high. They didn't chase clients; clients came to them, and they didn't advertise. That's the way our profession should be, but it has changed, along with the rest of our society. And though I know it's not hip to be retro, I prefer the days of "I like Ike", in the post-war presidency of Dwight Eisenhauer.

Well, by comparison in my simplistic approach to things, how does the profession look to those on I-95 in Florida who daily drive by a billboard that says, *"Who Can I Sue.com?"* (And, excuse me, but how does it look when sixty lawsuits are filed to overturn an election and every one of them is dismissed as baseless?)

One gets wistful looking back upon a seemingly more virtuous time.

Clarence Gifford was a very civic-minded attorney who volunteered with many community organizations. One day, he asked me into his office and explained that some of the leading corporate executives in the Rochester area planned to build an interfaith chapel on the grounds of the University of Rochester, along the river. (The University of Rochester was one of the first colleges in the country to have built a dedicated building as an Interfaith Chapel. They made history and completed the project in 1970. The Chapel is still there.)

Mr. Gifford had drafted a certificate for, as I recall, a religious corporation, and he asked me to take it to some of the people who had not yet signed, and then to take it to a Supreme Court Justice for a signature approving the certificate, which was required for that type of corporation.

I obtained the missing signatures and then headed for the Hall of Justice. Literally.

It never dawned on me to look at a list of Justices of the Supreme Court, and then *call* the chambers of one of them until I could get an appointment. Instead, I thought, I could just walk the ten or so blocks, crossing the river, and find a Justice.

Also, looking backward now, I realized that law school teaches substantive matters, but not so much practical applications. One has to learn that out in the field, so to speak. And so, being at the dawn of comprehension, I didn't really apprehend that there are trial level Supreme Court Justices and appellate justices who inhabited a loftier plain.

Inside the Hall of Justice, I approached one of the police officers at a welcome desk and told him I needed to see a judge. (I cannot even *imagine* doing that today!) He asked me the reason, and I told him, as if wandering around looking for a judge was normal.

If there is a way to distill naivete to its purest state, I was close to discovering it. You don't just walk into chambers of a sitting judge. You contact his or her clerk or secretary and you make an appointment.

The police officer, showing no warmth, and hiding ruthless guile, sent me to the Fifth Floor to one of the *Justices of the Appellate Division*. He was not just a Supreme Court Justice; he was on the appellate court which handled appeals from the eight-county Seventh Judicial District. (So many years later, my paralegal/bookkeeper wife, Liz, and I prepared over *three hundred* appeals to that body of five Justices, and I personally appeared to argue the appeals on a good number of them.)

Anyway, did I mention that in 1967 I looked like I was thirteen years old and had the innocent countenance of Walter E. Newman of *Mad Magazine*? (Too young to know it? Google it.)

The Justice's secretary welcomed me as she would a small child, and said the Justice would see me.

I told him what I needed and gave him the certificate of incorporation.

Now this is the part where I learned the lesson, and the part, which I obviously have never forgotten.

(I do not remember the names on the certificate, so I will use pseudonyms).

Looking at the certificate, frowning, the Justice said: "Now these signatures.... do you see where the name underneath the signature is typed?"

"Yes, Your Honor."

"Well, is it Henry Jones, or is it Henry J. Jones?"

"Um....."

"And see here, was it Mary R. Smith, or was it Mary Smith?"

Now the weight of tiny details massing together began to crush me and the Justice told me that in the future I needed to pay attention to them.

He signed the certificate and I took my first breath in the elevator on the way down to the first floor.

I was learning that in our infancy, small mistakes took on outsized consequences.

IT'S NOT EASY BEING A JUDGE

In 2015 I was asked by a Town Judge, who I will call Judge Simmons, to represent him in proceedings before the New York State Commission on Judicial Conduct. The Commission is an independent state agency charged with investigating allegations of judicial misconduct against New York state, county, town and village judges.

Unfortunately, there are many examples of judicial misconduct, some far more serious than others. The more serious violations of judicial ethics include such things as using the judge's office to obtain special treatment for friends or relatives; or accepting bribes, gifts, or other personal favors related to the judicial office; engaging in unwanted, offensive, or abusive sexual conduct, including sexual harassment or assault; or treating litigants, attorneys, judicial employees, or others in a demonstrably egregious and hostile manner; or intentional discrimination on the basis of race, color, sex, gender, gender identity, pregnancy, sexual orientation, religion, national origin, age, or disability.

The Commission can remove a judge from the bench in the more serious cases, usually those involving moral turpitude.

In my client's case the alleged transgressions were not of the more serious variety; they were procedural missteps. The formal written complaint alleged that he issued warrants of eviction and money judgments in two summary eviction proceedings without according the tenants an opportunity to be heard or reviewing all the supporting documents.

There were two complaints against Judge Simmons, one in each of two separate cases.

The facts were not in dispute, and, in fact, we stipulated to them.

In the first case the judge issued a warrant of eviction from a residential apartment against a couple without holding a hearing and taking testimony under oath, despite the fact that the tenants actually appeared in court while denying proper service of the papers. Their attorney acknowledged that the couple had received a notice of petition, but not the petition itself. During the proceeding, *the tenants acknowledged owing the rent demanded by the landlord and having defaulted on an existing payment agreement to pay the back rent.*

Judge Simmons, based upon his review of the court file and the tenants' acknowledgment of the unpaid rent, concluded that the landlord should be put in possession of the property. In rendering the judgment at that time, the judge, called *respondent* in the proceedings, was influenced by his belief based upon his long experience that a delay in the proceeding would only result later in increased judgment against the tenants for additional unpaid rent and late and legal fees. But he did acknowledge that he had not given the tenants a *formal* opportunity to be heard regarding a defense.

Judge Simmons issued a Warrant of Eviction and awarded the landlord a judgment for unpaid rent in the amount of $3,500. (Gee, would you agree the landlord had been somewhat tolerant?)

In the second case, as in the first, *the tenant acknowledged that she owed $1,950 in back rent.* Hearing that, Judge Simmons entered judgment and issued a warrant. When he did so, he did not know that as the tenant turned to the court clerk, she said she had consulted counsel and also claimed that she had not been properly served with a thirty-day notice. *She did not voice any of that to the judge.*

Before the Commission, Judge Simmons acknowledged that he did not give the tenant an opportunity to be heard regarding a defense, even though in their colloquy she had not mentioned it.

My client and I took the allegations seriously, but were not worried about removal from the bench. These were admitted as procedural oversights. And my client had a stellar and longstanding history on the bench.

But I asked myself, could we avoid the lesser penalty of public censure? Couldn't I present *the other side of the story*, as Paul Harvey used to say?

Very respectfully, these are the elements of the defense we asserted on behalf of the Judge:

- At the time of the complaints in 2015, Judge Simmons had been a Town Judge since 1971, *some 44 years*. (He would go on for *another four years*, making him one of the longest sitting jurists in New York State).
- During those years, *he had never been the subject of a complaint.*
- He was not an attorney.
- As was true of most town judges, his was a part-time position.
- Evictions are difficult, I told the Commission. I had researched the procedures required for a pluperfect eviction, and discovered that if every box were checked there were *thirty-three* procedural steps! They included such things as reviewing the notice of the petition and the allegations of the petition itself for completeness; was it properly

signed and notarized? was service of the papers on the tenant timely? was the affidavit of same properly signed and notarized? was the affidavit filed with the court in a timely manner? did the landlord give required thirty day notice *before* commencing the proceeding? were copies of all the above in the court's file? was there a written rental agreement? if so, was it filed with the court? was proper and timely notice of the court date given? was it *not less than* five days *nor more than* twelve?

I intimated to the Commission that a complaint before the Commission could conceivably arise if a judge missed compliance with any *one* of the thirty-three technical requirements.

- Judge Simmons' court was a NYS Thruway court, and it was an extremely busy court because of traffic tickets;
- for a number of years that Judge Simmons served, the judgeship for his counterpart judge (towns were supposed to have two judges) was *vacant*; this meant far more work for Judge Simmons;

And now, I asked Judge Simmons this series of questions and received these answers:

Q: "Could you estimate how many cases the Court might routinely hear on a given night?
A: "Sometimes, a *hundred*, including those which were submitted without appearances."
Q: "And on a typical evening, how many hours were you on the bench?"
A: "Three hours."
Q: "Would you typically take a recess?"

A: "No. I stayed on the bench the whole time."
Q: "Judge, if you had, say, one hundred cases and three hours to get through them, *how much time would that allow you for each case*?
A: "If I handled thirty cases each of the three hours?"
Q: "Yes."
A: "*Two minutes*."

To resolve the case, we agreed that an appropriate result would be the lowest form of penalty, namely public censure. (Fortunately, while the public can access the decisions of the Commission on line, the general public usually does not avail themselves of that opportunity. And, in this case, the publication of the decision was buried somewhere in the local newspaper.)

But Judge Simmons and I felt at the conclusion of the case that he had had his day in court. He had a chance to explain his side of the story. He had made it clear to the members of the Commission that even a conscientious, honorable and hardworking judge could easily find himself the subject of a complaint.

I felt that despite the censure, Judge Simmons had leveled the playing field somewhat. We left the Commission on Judicial Conduct feeling mutual respect, and in the pantheon of virtues resident in the law, respect is very near the warm center.

BUT SOMETIMES IT CAN BE FUN

I always liked going to Geneva City Court. In my first years the judge was Hon. Joe Caito, who was a delight. In retrospect, Danny DeVito reminds me of him.

Judge Caito had a heart and a sense of humor.

One of the first times I appeared before him I was able to work a deal with the Assistant DA. While Judge Caito was still in chambers we went in with my client and told the judge we had settled the case with a plea, if the Court would approve it. All pleas need the approval of the Judge.

Judge Caito liked lawyers, being one himself. The same may not be true for all judges, a very few of whom may have forgotten that before you can attain That Exalted Status of His Honor, you have to be a lowly attorney.

Anyway, we put the plea in; Judge Caito accepted it, and then said to my client:

"Now, you are getting a big break here, and there's only one reason for it. It's because your lawyer has done an excellent job for you. And it's only because of him that I've approved this plea."

It was all smoke, but I loved it, naturally, and, of course, hadn't done anything to deserve it. Such comments by judges were not so unusual back in the day, as they say, before we got all formal. (Though I confess that today some jurists will say to the attorneys after an in-court settlement, "Counsel, the Court appreciates your diligence in achieving this settlement.")

The client left while the ADA and I remained.

Judge Caito then looked at me and said, smiling, "Nice job. Where'd you get the sportcoat?"

As is true in so many walks of life, there are those who give the impression that your presence is an imposition; but also, those whose welcoming of you was the equivalent of a hug.

Reminds me of an aphorism I recently came across: "In a world where you can be anything, be kind."

TAKE HIM INTO CUSTODY! PLEASE!

Several years ago my partner Bob Zimmerman and I, and attorneys John Kennedy and Rob Gosper were golfing one Friday afternoon at Centerpointe in Canandaigua.

Bob was *completely unaware of it*, but one of his cases had been scheduled before a judge who shall remain nameless. He, the judge, was new to the bench, and, possibly, forgivably, a little anxious about his calendar. We've all been there, taking ourselves a little more seriously than we should. And this judge has proven to be one of the best in the years since.

But as I remember it, at the time, Bob received a call from the court clerk about the court appearance, asking where he was. Bob replied that no one had told him about it. Besides, he said "We're on the golf course."

We played on, unconcerned, except for routine and repeated horrible shots.

But a few minutes later *a police officer* showed up and tracked us down to whatever hole we were on! He had been sent by the judge to get Bob to court! (I hasten to add that Bob Zimmerman was and is well respected as a knowledgeable and dedicated attorney).

The officer was friendly enough, and probably had never had such an assignment.

Bob stuck to his guns, explaining to the officer that he had not scheduled an appearance that afternoon. John, Rob and I snickered like school girls. Then, like a Greek chorus, we begged the officer to take Bob into custody. It would have been perfect.

Had an arrest been made, we would certainly have taken a vote as to whether or not we should post bail.

But the officer diplomatically withdrew and John, Rob and I spent the rest of the afternoon complaining to Bob about lax law enforcement.

LAWYERS

ADVERSARIES CAN BE FRIENDS

All along the way in my career, I met such good lawyers. I revere them even now after all these years. We respected each other in the courtroom and outside it. They taught me by example, and even in the heat and contention of a trial, I believe there was a sense that we were participating in the greatest legal system in the history of the world. It was unspoken; we honored the Rule of Law. We were sometimes actors on a stage, but the backdrop was three-dimensional, telescoping back through centuries of principled thought and wisdom.

Along with their toughness and advocacy, they displayed courtesy, civility, respect, humility; these were the hallmarks of the lawyers with whom I worked.

The jaded and confrontational attitudes of actor-lawyers on television were for the most part absent in upstate Ontario County, New York, and in its surrounding jurisdictions.

Friendship was often readily apparent. Tom Gilmore, Esq., a fierce criminal defender from Palmyra, knew that our son, John, had been ill with a rare condition (erythema multiforme) when he was about two years old. For the next twenty years, Tom would say, "How's that son of yours?" (He was fine.)

Tom was larger than life itself, a top-shelf lawyer, a born defender, incisive, and a raconteur with a beating heart. He came into my office one day and said to my secretaries, "I'm Tom Gilmore. I need whiskey, and fresh horses for my men!" Tom was irrepressible. When his father, of the same name exactly, died, the newspapers reported it as *his* death.

When Farmington Town Judge Elwin Wasson told then ADA Bill Kocher (later to become county judge) that it wasn't really Tom, Kocher replied, "Oh? He got that adjourned, too??"

He is the same Tom Gilmore in the story below, "Did I have anything to drink at lunch, Mary?"

Max Cohen, another. Diminutive, somewhat mis-formed spine, razor sharp mind. Outgoing. Knowledgeable and experienced. He always found a way to remember the humanity; he always found a way to let in some light, and often, humor, in otherwise dark situations; the sharp arrows that might have wounded were rounded, made less stinging, if just as persuasive. Max delighted in telling the story of his representation of the family of a 300 pound decedent. As they took his casket out of the hearse at the cemetery to carry it toward the decedent's final resting place, the rotted bottom fell out and the decedent's remains thudded to the ground; a ghastly scene. (Lawyers acquire a sense of black humor; undoubtedly foster and promote it, too).

Bill Scott, one of the finest title attorneys I ever met, holder of the Distinguished Flying Cross, too modest to ever mention it.

John Britting, a lawyer's lawyer; none finer in real estate titles. Serious, fussy and respected by any lawyer with whom he ever dealt. A longstanding country lawyer if there ever was one.

Josh Barrett, who taught me a lesson. We were trying a difficult case where the emotion in our advocacy was evident. During a break, Josh came over to me and said, "John, we're getting a little crusty; we should dial it back a little." He was the better man that day, and I have never forgotten it. He is recently gone now, but I will never forget him; neither will his clients or the courts.

And Tom Trevett. We sat side by side in law school for three years. One day, his arm slipped off the table; he didn't know it. Shortly thereafter, he was diagnosed with multiple sclerosis. *He rose above it* to become President of the 2000-member Monroe County Bar Association and managing partner of his 20-member law firm. Toward the end, motorized wheelchair-bound, we often met for lunch. I loved him until the day he died in 2018, and still have his picture on my desk. He was a man for all seasons, and it was my privilege to be a part of his world.

And John Kennedy, who is mentioned elsewhere in this book. Riding in a golf cart with him on a Friday afternoon he said to me, "John, it doesn't get any better than this." John is gone now, but I will never forget him. I told him the last time I saw him on the day before he was to instruct his medical team to withdraw his life support apparatus, "John, we *will* meet again, maybe on a distant star."

And lady lawyers. Mary Jo Korona, Alexandra Burkett, Mary Lightsey, Jackie Ledgerwood, Teresa Pare, Meg Reston, Susan Jones; all fine advocates and pleasant to work with.

My partner, Bob Zimmerman, a warrior for the defense, who represented a young woman with two children, who was convicted in the death of two others. Whatever were the pressures which led her to those deaths, and to her conviction and sentence of thirty years to life, Bob has grieved it. She is still incarcerated. But several times a year for what seems like twenty or more years, Bob would rise at three in the morning, pick up her two children and drive to Bedford Hills prison so they could visit their mother, a model inmate. They don't teach that, and lawyers who have it don't talk about it. It emanates from wellsprings deep in the heart.

They are just some of many fine lawyers too numerous to mention who enriched me without knowing it. Some are gone now, but not really. Good and kindly deeds evoke their spirit.

"READY IF NOT REACHED"

One of the great local traditions in the law was "calendar call".

In civil litigation, once the pleadings have been exchanged and discovery has been completed, one of the attorneys files a so-called "Note of Issue" with the court clerk. That filing signals that the case is trial-ready.

Before computers took over the world like an alien automatons, the court clerks would compile a list of the cases which would be called for trial.

For years, Ontario County did not have a resident Supreme Court Justice; that is, one elected in the eight-county Seventh Judicial District. So to attend to the cases filed in Supreme Court a visiting justice would come to Ontario County for the so-called "term of court"; sort of like the so-called "circuit riders" of early American history, traveling judges going to specified jurisdictions to preside over cases.

On the first day of the arrival of a visiting justice, he or she would preside over "calendar call", when the cases would be called in order of their filing to set the trial priorities for the term.

The Ontario County Bar had a wonderful tradition: on the morning of calendar call flowers would be on the bench.

The lawyers with Supreme Court cases would appear to answer readiness for trial or state a reason why the case could not proceed.

Calendar call was an opportunity for lawyers to greet each other face-to-face; to shake hands; to chat about cases; and, especially, to renew old friendships.

Sometimes when his case was called, a jovial lawyer would call out "ready if not reached", and colleagues would chuckle, knowing that if your case was on the calendar you better be ready when it was reached, or have a good reason why not.

After calendar call the Bar would hold an informal luncheon at a nice restaurant for the visiting justice, the court clerk and those lawyers whose schedules would allow their attendance.

This warm tradition is gone now, replaced by the cold and impersonal digits of the electronic age.

I'm afraid it's a loss. Young attorneys will miss out on this gathering of colleagues, which was a sort of glue holding them together in a time-honored profession. We have become numb to dealing with faceless persons in many of our dealings, and the recent trend of having court appearance by Skype, or Scope, or whatever they call it, is a poor substitute for actually being in a courtroom. It's almost like a video game.

NIGHTMARES

Every lawyer lives with the fear that somewhere along the line he or she has made a mistake that is sleeping like a hibernating bear. The lawyer doesn't even know the mistake has occurred, but at some point, usually months or years later, it is discovered as he or she goes about the daily affairs. When it is presented it is unexpected; it is a rude and unwelcome surprise. It is always depressing; it is always threatening. It is the gnawing, galling realization of the risks of lawyerhood.

It is a specter that appears in even the best, the most diligent, ethical, conscientious law offices. It casts a dark shadow, haunting and implacable until it is met head-on, forthrightly; painfully.

The opportunities to miss something, to experience "law office failure", to omit doing some crucial act are limitless. Over my fifty-five year career, we handled thousands of real estate matters, hundreds of divorces, made thousands of criminal and family court appearances, wrote tens of thousands of letters and documents and real estate legal descriptions. In any one of these, the press of business, the distractions, the phone calls, the conferences with paralegals, the document preparation, the client consults, life itself, can cause that single instance of inattention that will burrow into a file drawer and simply wait, like a loaded mousetrap. And then one day somebody calls or writes to say, "We have a problem." Something didn't get filed. A deadline was missed. A court order awarding pension rights was not prepared, or was prepared, but not accepted by the pension administrator, then forgotten about. A legal description was erroneous. An heir is missing from a real estate chain of title. It's a long list.

The stories that follow provide some of the darker hues in the tapestry of a law office.

One of the valuable lessons I learned from those who raised me, my parents, teachers, boy scout leaders, church leaders......was to acknowledge your mistakes.

Malpractice is such a dirty word. When it becomes apparent, that is when the lawyer's honesty and ethics are tested. If a mistake has crept into a legal matter there is likely harm to someone, and it is the lawyer's *duty* to shoulder the aftermath, to make it right, to face the music.

From my twelve years on the 7th Judicial District Attorney Grievance Panel I know that the worst thing a lawyer can do when he or she comes face to face with his or her own fallibility is to stonewall it. Though it can be paralyzing, it won't get better with time; it won't go away. It doesn't age well.

In my fifty-five year career, I dealt with the hibernating bear on three occasions.

DEADLINE

As we'll see in another part of this book, at various times over our thirty-eight year partnership, Bob Zimmerman and I had invited a third lawyer to our practice. The first of these, whom I'll call Julie, came from an office where negligence was a specialty. Since I had limited experience with that field, I asked her if she would take over a case that had come to me. A client's son had been involved in a property auto accident, the fault of another driver. His truck was totaled. There were no injuries.

She took the file and I put it out of my mind.

I had no knowledge that a problem existed until it was too late: the associate failed to file a required pleading in a timely fashion, and the defense lawyer moved in Supreme Court to dismiss the case, with prejudice. The Court granted the motion, the death knell of that cause of action, with no recourse left to us.

Only when the clients asked me about delay in resolving the case did I learn from Julie that the case had been dismissed. She never told me about missing the deadline, the motion to dismiss, anything. She had stonewalled it. Bob and I got the aftermath.

I took immediate action. I met with the clients and told them that we had committed malpractice, and they should sue us.

At this time in our practice, we were not carrying malpractice insurance. On top of $12,000 annual library expense, malpractice insurance was another $6,000. We couldn't afford it.

(I chuckle when I read legal thrillers, where the lawyer is a self-deprecated "ham and egger"; Bob Zimmerman and I can relate to it).

The clients were long-time neighbors and friends; they said they would be satisfied if we would make the payments on a pickup truck to replace the one that had been damaged.

We did that, Bob and I. For more than thirty years, my wife, Liz, worked miracles with our law office expenses; with this case, we added to her burden, and every month she made the truck payments, $27,000 in all. Julie contributed nothing, though the mistake was hers alone. In truth, though, the ultimate responsibility was mine, for not monitoring the case.

Out of sight, out of mind, as they say, is not a good guiding principle for a law office, as I discovered.

It was painful, but it was the right thing to do. Ultimately, the good news is that our client suffered no harm. And would continue over later decades to come to our office.

THE COLD CLUTCHES OF IRS

Elsewhere in this book I have mentioned our client, Clara. As was seen, with the reference to the California real estate, her estate consisted of enough value to incur federal and estate taxes; the tax thresholds were much lower then than they are now. The taxes weren't.

Rarely over my career would I consent to act as executor of a client's estate. Some of the more acquisitive lawyers routinely drafted themselves in to client wills as the executor, and then took a fee for that, *and* for their legal work in the estate. That was not my practice. On the few occasions where I actually did serve as executor, it was usually a case where the client had no one else. On those estates, I took only one of the two fees. The practice of taking two fees was later forbidden in the absence of express written disclosures by the attorney to the client.

Clara's estate was one of the few where I did serve as executor. As part of my duties I prepared the federal estate tax return, calculated and paid the estate taxes, which were significant.

When the estate was wound up, all the assets were distributed to a series of charities, and on the estate tax return I took charitable deductions where appropriate.

Was there a mistake in there? *Yes.* Where there is a federal estate tax, the estate cannot be considered closed until a *closing letter* is received from

IRS. But at the same time there is some tension: the will bequests were to charitable institutions or colleges, and neither they nor I shared the same cosmic view of time as did IRS. It would be beneficial to disperse their gifts to them, rather than hold them while we waited for a closing letter.

About *three years* later, IRS wrote to me. One of the charitable deductions was to a cemetery in Connecticut. IRS disallowed the deduction, *because in the cemetery's charter there was no recital that it would bury indigent persons!* What??

Who would know that? Who would research it, on top of all the other moving parts of a large estate? Why would it take IRS three years to notify me of the disallowance of the charitable deduction, after all the estate assets had been distributed?

With interest and penalties, it was $15,000 out the window. We had no choice but to pay it, though it was unimaginably unfair, the epitome of lawyer danger; the severest test of ethical duty to clients.

Again, during the time of this matter we did not carry malpractice insurance.

I took IRS off my Christmas card list.

THE MISSING SECURITY INTEREST FILING

This one was pure negligence on my part. No escaping it.

We had handled a number of matters for my longstanding client, Rose. When she sold her manufactured home, she took back a $40,000 note. To secure it, a so-called Uniform Commercial Code filing was made in Albany. It was the same as if one bought a car and financed it through a bank; the bank lends the money and takes back a promissory note, then files the lien, or security interest, in Albany

I prepared the note and filed the security interest in Albany.

But in addition to the UCC filing, a copy of the promissory instrument forming the basis of the obligation, the $40,000 note, needed to be identified, and it wasn't.

When the owner of the manufactured home decided to sell a few years later, he decided that since there was no valid lien in Albany on it he would simply *not pay* the balance of the $40,000. I'm sure his name is listed somewhere on The Honesty Registry.

Our client was out the $40,000, less whatever payments the owner had already paid.

Facing the depressing music, I met with Rose and told her she should sue us. Meanwhile, since we now had malpractice insurance, I immediately notified our insurer and related all the necessary facts, alerting them to the possible claim, and acknowledging my error. In truth, Rose would never have suffered a loss on this.

But Rose, bless her, would not consider pursuing a claim, despite my pressing her to do so. Life had treated her kindly; she didn't need the money and she valued our service to her over decades in which we represented her. We had shown many kindnesses to her, and much deserved respect.

When she was gone, her grandson was just as gracious as she had been. We handled her estate without fee.

No friend, no client, no family member could have been more kind, more forgiving, than Rose. One, such as myself in this case, who receives an undeserved kindness never forgets it.

Rose is among the lightest, most agreeable pastels in the tapestry of our legal journey, along with one of the darker hues.

LUNCH WITH BOB

One of the lighter hues.

For at least two decades, Bob, Liz and I went to lunch together. For long stretches we went either to Countryside Restaurant in Clifton Springs or Park Place in Farmington.

It was always something to look forward to, one of the highlights of the day.

It was a chance to tell our individual stories: Bob's criminal law cases, my real estate challenges, divorces, whatever.

It seems Bob usually had a hopeless criminal case, and Liz and I tried to be helpful: "Bob, we know you have a trial coming up, and we've been thinking about your opening to the jury."

"Yeah?"

"Wanna hear it?"

"Yeah."

"Ladies and Gentlemen, my name is Bob Zimmerman and I represent the defendant in this case. Let us pray."

We know this was helpful, as of course we intended it to be.

CLEAR THE COURTROOM!

Now, this is indelicate, but I mention it only because it could only happen to a country lawyer.

I was not present at this event, so this is hearsay, augmented by devilish imagination.

My partner, Bob Zimmerman, was appearing in a local town night court with an elderly gentleman who was appearing to answer for some minor alleged transgression.

The gentleman's daughter stood beside him, with Bob, before the judge on his elevated bench.

While Bob was addressing the court, the daughter said, "OH, DAD!!!"

The elderly gentleman had.... um.....lost control of his bowels.

The judge, wondering about a lapse in the dialogue with Bob, heard Bob say something like, "Um, Your Honor, we need a recess".

Puzzled, the judge peered over the bench and then, with zero hesitation, said "CLEAR THE COURTROOM!!!"

As I have said to Bob many times over the years, "You wanted to be a lawyer."

HAM AND EGGERS

The phrase has many meanings, but to my partner Bob Zimmerman and I it jokingly refers to a couple of lawyers, ordinary guys, plugging away day to day. Since our practice never included negligence work (automobile crashes), we did not receive the large fees that go with that kind of practice. In a matter of months from the very beginning of my practice I knew I would not handle such cases. The lawyers spoke of "questionable liability, but *good injuries*." (I don't ascribe a kind of callousness to those lawyers; it was just a manner of speech. And for those who are severely injured it is lawyers who do what can be done to help them economically. It's just that it wasn't my cup of tea).

So Bob, practicing almost exclusively in criminal law, and myself handling real estate, wills and estates, divorces, Family Court, general business and municipal work, patched together a successful practice. Not rich, but enough to pay the bills and help support the family.

Recently, when the end of our practice together was visible on the horizon, we agreed that our practice gave us rich personal experiences and wonderful opportunities to make a difference in some way in our world.

For a couple of ham and eggers.

PARALEGALS

―――――― "HOW CAN I HOLD YOU?" ――――――

In our country practice, we used a broad definition of the term, "paralegal". Not to diminish the efforts of those who have attended college paralegal courses, in our country practice we considered *anyone who worked with us* a paralegal. I suspect our definition of the term is more apt as applied to our office than it would be in a large firm, or, certainly, in a litigation firm.

No license or registration is currently offered for paralegals in New York State, and no degree is currently required to serve as a paralegal. There are no statewide mandatory certifications for them in New York. According to its website, The Empire State Alliance of Paralegal Associations is attempting to put through policies requiring training in a postsecondary paralegal studies program accredited by the American Bar Association (ABA). But so far, I know of none.

If you Google "duties of a paralegal", the U.S. Bureau of Labor Statistics lists the following:

- Investigate and gather the facts of a case
- Conduct research on relevant laws, regulations, and legal articles
- Organize and maintain documents in paper or electronic filing systems
- Gather and arrange evidence and other legal documents for attorney review and case preparation
- Write or summarize reports to help lawyers prepare for trials

- Draft correspondence and legal documents, such as contracts and mortgages
- Get affidavits and other formal statements that may be used as evidence in court
- Help lawyers during trials by handling exhibits, taking notes, or reviewing trial transcripts
- File exhibits, briefs, appeals and other legal documents with the court or opposing counsel
- Call clients, witnesses, lawyers, and outside vendors to schedule interviews, meetings, and depositions

That list is heavy on the litigation aspects of a law office, and mostly inapplicable to our office. But many of the same *type* of duties certainly applied to our practice. So, for example, with our wills and estates, our secretaries prepared the documents such as wills, which the lawyer drafted, proof read them, often challenged or inquired about parts of the same, contacted the clients, arranged tracking for signatures, did all the filing. They prepared documents, such as powers of attorneys and health care proxies, for the lawyer's review. Frequently, they researched administrative issues like filing requirements and fees; but also pointed out the need for legal research in specific areas, such as in the Surrogate's Court Procedure Act, the Estates, Powers and Trusts law, the Real Property Law, the Real Property Actions and Proceedings Law and the Domestic Relations Law concerning adoptions. We frequently exchanged printouts of excerpts of certain laws, and, in truth, collaborated on them.

Our considerable institutional knowledge resided in the collective memories of Teri, Janice and Liz, as well as their recognition of clients past and present.

In our real estate, legal descriptions and title examinations were done by myself, but most of the other papers were prepared by our secretaries, Janice and Teri.

In short, if you were in our office, you were a paralegal, with or without a degree; but always, with real world experience.

At Zimmerman & Tyo, that kind of experience was invaluable. And other experience. For example, our paralegals developed telephone skills:

"Attorney's office. How can I hold you?"

"Attorney's office. Happy Birthday."

"Good morning. Atturkey's office."

"Have a Merry Christmas and a Happy New York."

"Is this the person to whom I'm speaking?"

Oh, yes; we had a lot of fun, along with the work.

The warm core of our paralegal staff (more like family) consisted of Teri on wills, powers of attorney, estates, real estate and municipal matters; Janice on real estate and Bob's criminal calendar; Liz, our bookkeeper, and, with me, on matrimonials and appeals.

These three professionals worked together in our office for over thirty years. In a society where "a job for life" is an anachronism, they were an exception. And before them, Lucille A. Dobbler, who for fifteen years taught us all.

LIKE DRILL SERGEANTS

Now, a confession. I know how important it is that the signed names agree with the typed names, but, in truth, over the years it has been my paralegals who have zeroed in on such things to insure professional accuracy. Where my gaze dreamily floats over a document requiring my signature, they conduct a supervisory review something like that of a drill sergeant. On any given day in a law office, any law office, an attorney might sign his or her name thirty times. Each time is an opportunity to overlook some detail or other.

I often told clients: "Janice (or Teri) treat me like a kindergartener."

I WAS NEVER ALONE

So, while I'm at it, I need to mention that looking back over my fifty-five year career as a lawyer, I realize that I was never alone. Always, there was someone by my side whose abilities surpassed my own, who enhanced our office, who welcomed clients and attended to their needs.

Those someones were the paralegals with whom I worked side by side. By my count beginning with my three and a half years with Remington, Gifford, Wiley and Williams, there were at least some twenty-two of them, who were, from the beginning of my career to its end, a steadfast and reliable presence in my life in the law. When I count my blessings, they along with the others who shepherded me through the wondrous variety and challenges of the law, are foremost in my mind.

A BRIEF DIGRESSION:

ON THE WAY TO SHORTSVILLE

EARLY CAREER IN A NUTSHELL

Before I get to the criminal cases, a brief narrative of my journey to my country law practice.

I was raised in what is now called "The South Wedge" in Rochester, a great place then and now. After graduating from John Marshall High School, I graduated from SUNY-Albany with a degree in history/English.

The law school was really never in my sights. But just three months from graduation from SUNY with an intended career as a teacher, and already having done my student teaching, I accompanied a friend to Albany law school, where he had to drop off some papers. On the spur of the moment, I submitted an application and gained admittance, graduating in 1967. At Albany Law School I learned deep respect for The Rule of Law, for the value of debate and dialogue, for ethics, for the critical importance of preparation in all things, for honest and principled argument and for the equanimity inherent in legitimate opposing views.

As mentioned earlier, my career began with Remington, Gifford, Wiley & Williams, Attorneys, in Rochester, New York in 1967. Within three years, though, my practice in Ontario County had grown to the point I needed to tend to it there. So I reluctantly left Remington, Gifford and took a position with an attorney in Canandaigua. While there, I was tutored by one of the best paralegals ever to walk into an office. Lucille A. Dobbler taught me enough that I had some confidence that I could start a solo practive. I opened my first solo office in Shortsville, located over what was then Security Trust Company, and with me came the young lady who would build my practice: Barbara Berdzinski was early twenties-something. During occasional slow times in our first couple of years, we played euchre. Some fifty years later we are still friends and with our spouses meet two or three times a year. And, my good luck streak continuing, Lucille joined us for another fifteen or so years!

One day in 1970 Max Morris, a longstanding fine country lawyer with a home office in Manchester, pulled me aside at the Courthouse. "I'd like you to take over my practice," he said, to my great surprise. "But," he added, "I'm leaving for Florida *next week*, and I also want you to buy my house." He proposed that for a period of one year we would transition the practice to me. We were partners for that one year, sharing fees on an amicable basis.

I did buy Max's house, and because he loved to prepare income tax returns, Barbara and I worked until late in the evenings doing the same. In time, I would refer the clients to accountants, but not until we had made initial contacts with them.

In a short time after Max retired, I sold the house and practiced out of the Shortsville office until 1986, when with my law partner Bob Zimmerman and two other partners we bought the former Papec Office Building, which had been utterly vacant for twelve years. We borrowed $180,000 and rehabilitated the building. Over the next decade Bob and I would buy out the other partners. Eventually, we sold the building to the Village of Shortsville.

Early in the above time line, around 1970, I would start wearing The White Hat.

THE CRIMINAL MATTERS

WHITE HAT, BLACK HAT

THE WHITE HAT

Around 1970 I took a position with the Ontario County District Attorney's Office.

I covered all the Thruway courts (Phelps, Manchester, Farmington, Victor), Canandaigua City Court and several other town courts. No lawyer, no matter how energetic, could cover all those courts today; the avalanche of cases in each approaches the point of being overwhelming.

The town courts required exclusively evening court appearances, except for occasional Saturday jury trials, while the City Court appearances were every morning.

It was as an Assistant District Attorney that I gained trial experience. In the 60's and 70's law enforcement seemed to wink at driving while intoxicated. Jim Harvey, who would later become District Attorney and then County Court Judge, and I changed that. We were young and brash. We prosecuted DWIs with zeal, believing that the time had come for the danger to be taken seriously.

My first DWI trial and conviction was *People v. Warren Davison* in Victor Town Court. I saved the trial transcript, and still have it. It was the first of many such trials.

Shortly into my career as a prosecutor the breathalyzer was introduced. Before it, law enforcement had to rely on urine tests (the officers disliked it; they had to observe, and there were times when they were peed upon), or blood tests (also disliked; had to subpoena medical personnel, who didn't like it, either). The breathalyzer changed everything. It was pioneered in Chemung County.

I prosecuted the first breathalyzer trial in Ontario County.

Prosecution of such a case required a keen knowledge of evidence, much preparation and good organizational skills. As a prosecutor, I needed testimony from the arresting officer, a chemist from Albany to establish the scientific principles underlying the machine and a technician from Troop E to establish the proper testing, calibration and maintenance of the machine. Typically, a DWI jury trial would start at 6:00 o'clock in the evening and last until about 3:00 the next morning. After the trial I would usually meet with the police officers at The Bunkhouse on Route 21 along the tracks in Manchester, just north of Bliss Shurfine Market. It was torn down sometime in the 70's, but in its day it served railroaders with good, wholesome food and coffee.

During my three and a half years as an Assistant District Attorney, I learned my way around a courtroom.

And around Ontario County. I was young and restless. So after my family had retired for the night I often called the Sheriff's Office to send a patrol car over to pick me up. Many nights I would ride with a deputy from ten or eleven in the evening until two or three in the morning.

They liked to put out over the radio: "I got the ADA with me." For them, it was a rarity. For me, it was, frankly, a thrill, along with a learning experience. Sometimes they let me work the radio, like a kid with a walkie-talkie.

During this time I gained respect for the work police officers do, and, frankly, for the restraint they displayed in unpleasant situations.

THE BLACK HAT

After the ADA years, I resigned in order to have a little more family time. As it turned out, I would wear The Black Hat, taking criminal defense cases for the next thirty or so years.

CAN NAGS BE RACEHORSES?

My trial theory was no, they can't.

My client came in asking that I represent him in an animal cruelty case in Hopewell Town Court.

Someone had complained that he had several malnourished horses, a violation of the New York State Agricultural and Markets Law. That statute defines cruelty: as "every act, omission, or neglect, whereby unjustifiable physical pain, suffering or death is caused or permitted". The complaint alleged that the horses were thin, probably underfed and looked in poor overall condition. Obviously, inferred the complaint, they had not been properly cared for.

We denied the charge and asked for a jury trial.

The trial was held at night at the Hopewell Town Hall before Hon. Roland Poole, one of the kindest, most humble and fair town judges who ever took the bench. For routine appearances we used to meet in his kitchen, as was true with many town judges across Ontario County before we got all formal. (If there was any doubt that the justice courts were the courts closest to the people, appearing in the judges' homes was proof of it).

With all due respect to the Agricultural and Markets Law, and to the cause of proper care of animals, I decided that in this case the best defense was to make a mockery of the charges. *I would compare my client's horses to racehorses.*

After the People's case, I called my client, the owner of the horses. We established that he had owned horses most of his life. He understood horses. He had the skill and knowledge to care for them. He had never mistreated them or been accused of doing so. In fact, he loved horses and kept these just so they would have a home.

My direct examination established: His horses were old: though he could not state their actual age, he would estimate something between 15 and 20 years. Yes, their teeth were worn. Yes, they might have a touch of arthritis. Yes, they looked a little droopy. Yes, their eyes were a little hollow. Yes, they had gray hairs around their muzzle and eyes. Yes, their coats were a little dull. Yes, their appetites were a little less than when they were younger. And yes, they might have dropped a little weight.

And then, the question I couldn't wait to ask, and couldn't stifle a smile as I did so: "Are they racehorses?"

And just for the hell of it, I showed him a picture of a racehorse and asked him if his horses looked like that. He chuckled a little, shook his head a little and in his folksy voice quietly said, "No, they are a little too old for that."

Now the jury was smiling.

I called my second, and final, witness. Billy was a friend of my client. He was a horse lover and generally assisted my client in their care of the horses in question. He was a round-faced gentle soul, affable, with an open countenance and a winning, if simple, smile. It wouldn't be kind to suggest that he lacked intelligence, but his manner of speech, his happy cooperation and his enthusiastic unadorned answers to my questions gave a hint that he may have had some deficits. It would be impossible for him to conjure false answers.

Any jury would immediately feel the same affection for him as they would a child.

I had pictures of the horses showing nothing more than that they were a little swayed back and thin, consistent with their age.

"Billy, I show you this item marked for identification as Defense Exhibit 1, and ask if you can identify it."

In one of the most hilarious exchanges I ever had with a witness, his face lit up, his eyebrows raised up, he looked at the picture, sat up straight and he smiled.

"HORSES!" He said in a loud voice.

I laughed. Judge Poole laughed. The jury laughed.

The not guilty verdict was no surprise. It concluded one of the most enjoyable trials I ever had, and even today, some thirty or more years later, I think of Billy every time I see a horse.

DUCK

One night while I was with the DA's office I was riding with Deputy Leon Mills, who had parked the patrol car in the parking lot of Schafer's tire repair garage just west of the Village of Clifton Springs. Suddenly, a car came speeding up the hill, passing our location and heading west on County Road 13. Deputy Mills gave chase.

At the intersection of east/west County Road 13 and north/south County Road 7, the driver made a wild right turn onto County Road 7, followed immediately by a second wild right turn onto Stevens Street, doubling back east into the Village.

He overcompensated the second turn, and in the process blew out both tires on the passenger side of the vehicle. Undeterred, and with us in hot pursuit, he drove as fast as his vehicle would allow, looking like a roman candle in the darkness as sparks flew off the rubberless steel rims on the passenger side of the vehicle.

Deputy Mills said, "Get on the radio and tell LeRoy we're coming into the Village, and to set up a roadblock." Like a kid with a toy, I made the call to dispatch.

Coming into the village, as we approached the Kendall Street intersection, Clifton Springs Police Chief Steve Le Roy was standing at the edge of the pavement with a shotgun, his patrol car positioned to block both lanes, not entirely. There was a slot to the right where Chief LeRoy stood.

The car we were pursuing never slowed; instead it headed for a narrow patch of pavement around Chief Le Roy's vehicle. The Chief stepped backward in anticipation as the vehicle approached.

I can still see Chief Le Roy today: with his legs spread shoulder-wide he made three controlled and deliberate hops, each time aiming at the front wheel of the car we were chasing. On the third hop, he fired the shotgun. I saw it coming and heard it; I hit the floor.

The driver continued a couple more blocks, then was finally forced over and was apprehended. Need I say he had been drinking? He was taken into custody without any struggle. The police response was controlled and professional. Later, I wondered if I had been one of the officers could I have exhibited the same detachment from the heat of the chase.

This was one of many episodes where I gained respect for the work police officers do, and, frankly, for the restraint they displayed in tense situations.

My skill at ducking has been invaluable on the golf course.

DID I HAVE ANYTHING TO DRINK AT LUNCH, MARY?

Elsewhere in this book I've mentioned my colleague, Tom Gilmore, Esq.

He and I were trying a driving while intoxicated case before Hon. Charlie Rose, Victor Town Judge, *and a jury*, on a Saturday.

Judge Rose was a school administrator by profession, but also an elected Town Judge. He was a scholar, and was for a time the President of the New York State Magistrates Association. An attorney always needed to be on his toes in Judge Rose's court because he was one of the keenest non-attorney judges anywhere. Faithfully, he read the so-called *advance sheets*. Back in Judge Rose's time, New York decisional law was bound into numbered volumes; the green paper back advance sheets contained the very latest decisional law before there were enough cases to fill a bound volume. So if one wanted to check for any late decisions, he or she would turn to the advance sheets. (Nowdays, one clicks on something.)

Most of the DWI cases I tried before Judge Rose were in the evenings; but this one, with Tom Gilmore, was on a Saturday.

As I've hinted elsewhere, Tom was one of the people who seemed larger than life. He had a pleasant, deep voice, an easy, devilish smile and a hearty laugh. But, make no mistake, he was a lethal advocate who took on the most difficult, unpopular and often ugly criminal defense cases anywhere.

This particular Saturday, I put my case on in the morning session. It usually involved the arresting officer, and, if it was a breathalyzer case, also the tech sergeant, a chemist from Albany and anyone else who might have pertinent evidence; perhaps, a witness to errant driving. In cases where there was no breathalizer test, the damning evidence came from the arresting officer, who usually testified to the intoxication giveaways: slurred speech, flushed face, unsteady on feet, unable to recite the alphabet *backwards* (I always wondered whether *I* could do it, *sober*), unable to walk a straight line, etc. With such evidence a breathalyzer wasn't necessary; so-called common law intoxication could be established, subjectively, through these indicators.

But with the advent of the breathalyzer, prosecutors would introduce both "plain intoxication" through the arresting officer's observations, and intoxication based upon the scientific machine.

A word about the machine: it measured the amount of alcohol present in a person's deep lung air, the so-called *alveolar* air. When a person blew into the mouthpiece, his breath passed through one of two so-called bubbler tubes; one of those contained a known and constant liquid solution; the other, through which the person's air passed, *changed color* and the degree of change in the color was compared with the color of the other, fixed, tube. The degree of change gave a reading of the amount of alcohol in the alveolar air, and, thus, the blood.

If the evidence was presented fully and properly, the machine survived many challenges: the machine was not scientifically reliable; it was not properly calibrated; the administering officer lacked the proper training; only one test was performed; the defendant's medical condition, such as a gastro issue or high ketone levels could affect the reading; certain over-the-counter medications could give a "false positive" reading; electric or radio frequency interference could affect the reading. All these challenges were made, but in time, the breathalyzer established its reliable scientific pedigree.

Juries had a child-like faith in the breathalizer. So did I, because Jim Harvey, the other Assistant District Attorney at the time, and I, left a retirement dinner one night and drove up to the State Police barracks on Route 332 to take the test. I was .06; Jim was .07. At the time, the standard for intoxication was .12. Forever afterward I knew, from what I had had to drink that night how much alcohol one had to consume to reach .12; it was a considerable amount, so I never doubted the validity of a test.

Of course, not to lose sight of other aspects of the case, the police testimony must first have established probable cause for the arrest; crossing the center line, crossing the fog line, driving too slowly, weaving, speeding, no lights, etc.

Back to the trial. We broke for lunch.

Now, Tom was sometimes accompanied by his lovely wife, Mary, at trials. She had been present at the morning session; they left for lunch together.

Back in court for the afternoon session, Tom called his first witness, the defendant, who protested his innocence; he had had only two drinks, he said.

I remember the following colloquy as if it were yesterday:

Judge Rose: Call your next witness.
Tom: I call **Mary Gilmore**.
(Mary approached and Judge Rose administered the oath. Now Tom had my attention, especially since I thought I saw a twinkle in his eye.)
Tom: Mary, do you know me?
Mary: Yeeess, Tom, I know you.
Tom: How do you know me, Mary?
Mary: *I'm your wife*, Tom.
Tom: Ok. Now, Mary, did we go to lunch today?
Mary: Yes, Tom.
Tom: And Mary, at lunch did I have anything to drink?
Mary: Yes, Tom, you had two drinks.
Tom: Alcoholic drinks?
Mary: Yes, Tom.
Tom: Thank you, Mary.
Tom: No further questions, Your Honor.
Me (smiling): Your Honor, I have no questions.

Now, Tom, that rascal, was trying to make the point that if he could have the same number of drinks as his client, and, notwithstanding the same, perform normally back in court, not showing any signs of intoxication, the same could be said for his client's driving.

It was a nice try, and for me, a memorable one; but the jury wasn't convinced; rather, it was convinced beyond a reasonable doubt of the defendant's guilt.

Looking backwards, it seems now to me that in those earlier days of my career, and earlier, we lawyers could have a little fun. One Victor Town Court story that made the rounds was that back in the day when lawyers could *smoke* in court one lawyer would run a very thin wire down a cigar, and light it up with exaggerated motions as the prosecutor opened to the jury. The wire would hold the ashes in place, and as the trial wore on, the jury was mesmerized by the growing length of the ashes, their attention distracted from the prosecutor's blather.

It seems we lawyers would see each other year after year in town and village courts, exchange greetings, swap stories, joke around a little. But as the years passed the court calendars became more crowded, the cases seemed more serious and more formality crept into the proceedings. More than anything, with the calendars becoming increasingly crowded, the focus was on getting your case(s) called so you could be home. Night court sessions usually started at 7:00 and it was not unusual that your case would not be called for an hour or two. I couldn't wait to get home from these night appearances, which were often three nights a week. To get my case(s) called, I developed an artificially sad face to show the judge, so pathetic that would make you cry; it seldom worked.

Tom Gilmore is gone, now, but those who knew him respect his memory, his legacy as a stand-up defense warrior and his irrepressible spirit.

THE ASSIGNED FELONY CASES

ASSIGNED COUNSEL - THE BLACK HAT

After about three years as an Assistant District Attorney, I left the position and started taking cases assigned to me by the judges of the courts. We had a so-called assigned counsel system then, whereby when a defendant could not afford to retain private counsel, the judge would contact the Assigned Counsel Administrator. His office would then take an application by the defendant to verify his indigent status, and when that was established, an attorney with criminal law experience would be assigned to the case.

There was no actual assigned counsel office; the attorney assigned to the case would utilize whatever resources he had in his private office; his own staff; his own library; his own materials and equipment. If he needed an investigator, he had to make application to the court for authority to engage the services of the investigator, and the parsimonious amount usually awarded did not foster a deep dive into the evidence. The assigned attorney would keep track of his time and, when the case was closed, submit a voucher for payment. The hourly rates were very low, and capped at a certain level unless a judge approved a higher fee.

Over the years the system worked well, but there came a time when the state mandated that counties establish a so-called Public Defender Office, and that is what is in place now. It is a counterpart to the District Attorney's Office; it is bricks and mortar, equipment, library, supplies, investigators and a number of full and part-time attorneys to match the DA's office.

FIRST ASSIGNED FELONY CASE: A MURDER

I hadn't been out of the DA's office but a very short time when Judge Robert Kennedy assigned me to defend Joseph Pyclik.

Mr. Pyclik was accused of shotgunning Robert Heavey to death in Heavey's home in Victor.

Mr. Pyclik's story was that he was new to the Rochester area. He went to a bar there, and happened to make the acquaintance of Mr. Heavey, who happened to invite him to his home, where he stayed overnight. (It was never mentioned in the proceedings then, but nowadays someone would say: "It was a gay bar.")

Anyway, in the morning, Mr. Pyclik's penis hurt! He had been sexually abused! He had to escape! He grabbed a shotgun from a closet and was backing away from a confrontation with Mr. Heavey when he tripped over the raised fireplace threshold. The shotgun discharged, killing Mr. Heavey.

It was an unbelievable story. You can't make this stuff up. But as I jokingly tell my law partner, Bob Zimmerman, who does almost exclusively criminal law: You wanted to be a lawyer.

What did Mr. Pyclik do after the shooting? He took a record player from Heavey's home, and his vehicle, and drove away. Yes, the inconsistency was glaring.

I do not recall the manner in which he was apprehended. Probably someone spotted the car.

And now, I entered the case as assigned counsel; I was not exactly a rookie, given my experience as a part-time assistant district attorney. But I had never handled a felony case.

With this case, I learned the burden of defending someone accused of a major crime. It is a journey through an uncertain and sometimes shifting landscape. It is monumental self-doubt. It is warfare between what can reasonably be presented to a jury, and what is outlandish. It is motions, court appearances, jail visits, lists of witnesses and exhibits; it is psychology; it is show business. It is paranoia. It is the relentless, demanding focus on opening and closing statements. It is months. It is sleepless nights. It is dread of a bad outcome for which you haven't the slightest responsibility aside from your own professional duties. And it is insistence that it take precedence over other law office matters; so it is in addition to everything else, a balancing act.

And throughout, you are alone. No one sits as so-called *second chair*. And no psychologist helps with jury selection. No investigator sits besides you.

More than anything, it is the curse of ethical lawyers: *you can't change the facts*.

But, I walk into the courtroom with Joseph Pyclik, and we sit together at the defense table, face to face with one of the sternest, intense, task-master judges on the bench; a former prosecutor, unmarried, rigid, deeply devout, cold, righteous and abrupt. In his role as a Family Court Judge he was fond of saying: "You know, I can take your children away from you."

We start jury selection, an important part of any case, where the lawyers have an opportunity to examine proposed jurors in an attempt to weed out those who cannot, or will not be fair. It is guesswork; it is intuition. Today, there are so-called jury selection consultants, who supposedly can read a juror on his or her answers to the voir dire (to tell the truth) questions posed by the court and attorneys, to interpret demeanor, facial expressions, posture and the like.

In my career I never used one, for two reasons: first, the state would not pay for it, and private clients could not afford it. Secondly, forgive me, but I've never been convinced that it is a step above voodoo.

Before long, I have the impression that the judge in his tone of voice and facial expressions is signaling disapproval of my decisions about the jury panel. I take a big breath and summon whatever feather-light gravitas

I possess and say to His Honor: "Your Honor, I take exception to the fact that you are making faces while I am addressing the jury".

With that, I have thrown down the gauntlet. Maybe I am crazy, but I'm not going to get pushed around. Respect is one thing; being obsequious is another. Respect is a two-way street.

Your Honor: "I don't know what you mean." I think he did, and I had set a tone for the rest of the trial, and maybe for the part of my career where I would be a defense lawyer.

The prosecutor opens. Now in our system, the prosecutor, because he is the first to address the jury, gets to outline the evidence he expects to present; he's planting seeds.

Then, after all the evidence is in from both sides, defense counsel gives a closing statement, a summation, to the jury. That means the prosecutor has an advantage: he knows what the defense lawyer has said to the jury and can attack it, rebut it. The defense lawyer does not have that advantage, and has no opportunity to rebut it. The prosecution gets the first and last crack at the jury.

Now, there are two kinds of opening statements to a jury. One is a hedge: "Ladies and Gentlemen...." and you tell them that an indictment is not proof of the commission of a crime; it is only an allegation. The proof comes from the witnesses. Keep an open mind. Remember the hallmarks of our system of justice: the presumption of innocence and the requirement of proof beyond a reasonable doubt, etc., etc.

This is the statement you make when you are *not sure where the case is heading*, or where you are *not sure you are going to put your client on the stand*.

But this kind of statement allows the prosecutor's opening to hang in the air, like vapor for the jury to breathe in. The generic defense opening does nothing to counter the District Attorney's dramatically damning remarks.

The other kind of opening statement involves a risky commitment. It is the statement where you lay out your side of the story. *Once you tell it, you are committed*; you will not be able to back up, change it, if the trial evidence and witness testimony, or even your own client, betrays you.

This type of opening is an attempt to deflate the prosecution's case in advance.

And in this case, Pyclik, that's the opening I gave, with a straight face.

After the prosecution's case is in, I take the leap, jump off the cliff, and put Mr. Pyclik on the stand. This is a gamble. There are cases where you would duct tape your client and tie him to the chair to keep him from testifying because he can only kill himself. Keeping him off the stand, though, is a gamble, too, because no matter that the judge tells the jury that it can draw no inference from the defendant's silence, the jury can't help wondering: if he's innocent, why won't he tell us his side of the story? It's a Hobson's Choice.

But in this case, The Barely Believable Story of Joseph Pyclik is presented to the jury. As the story unfolds, I am rapt with studied credulity, head tilted, nodding in understanding, wrinkled brow, pursed lips. Laurence Olivier couldn't have done a better job of acting.

We proceed. Pyclik is facing 25-to-life for the murder.

Unbelievably, and probably only because the jury takes pity on the defendant because of his child-like lawyer, it finds him guilty of Criminally Negligent Homicide, which carries a maximum sentence of *four years*! He gets that, plus seven, consecutively, for stealing the record player and the car. (Many defendants are not graduates of The School for the Gifted).

My career as a killer defense lawyer has been launched. Kinda.

——— A DIGRESSION: THE IMPORTANCE OF DEFENSE COUNSEL ———

Every criminal defense lawyer is always, always asked: "How can you defend someone you know is guilty?" Or, "How can you try to get him off, when you know he's guilty?"

It's a good question, an understandable question. My answer has always been that *a defense lawyer does not have to believe his client*. He or she is not the trier of fact; that's the function of the jury. The defense attorney's role is to be an advocate, not in defense of the crime, not in justification of it, *but in the quest for a fair trial*. To counterbalance the power and might and resources of the state. In the average case the prosecution's assets can be likened to a powerful locomotive; the defense's, a VW microbus.

Nevertheless, it is defense counsel's role to do what can be done to insure that whatever is the final result, it is achieved with fairness. Most prosecutors and law enforcement officers are honorable men and women. But it is naive to believe that there are no overreaching, overzealous participants in the criminal justice system; that there are no phony scientific tests; that there are no untruthful witnesses, or witnesses who have been coached to remember what in fact they never knew or saw; that evidence doesn't disappear *before it gets to the DA*, as was the case in my most troubling and fascinating case, People v. Coleates, as we will see. (I do not suggest for a moment any unseemly actions, ever during my career, by anyone in the Ontario County District Attorney's Office, for whom I have the greatest respect.)

There are some wonderfully dedicated lawyers in New York City and elsewhere who work for The Innocence Project, a non-profit organization committed to exonerating wrongly-convicted people through the use of DNA testing and newly-discovered or suppressed evidence. According to Wikipedia, the work of the Project has, since its formation in 1992, freed more than 350 wrongly-convicted people, largely, but not exclusively, based on DNA analysis, including twenty persons who spent time on death row, and the finding of one hundred fifty real perpetrators.

Power corrupts. This truism sometimes has application in the courtrooms. A stout defense is the only leveling influence. Defense lawyers are as much a part of The Rule of Law as are prosecutors, and as valuable to it. Without them, a prosecution can be a runaway train; it has no brake as it builds its momentum, rushes inexorably to conviction.

It is a worthy investment of time to read the story of *Gideon v. Wainwright*, where a poor, uncounseled defendant was wrongfully convicted of stealing a few cans of soda and sentenced to five years in prison. From his cell, he wrote a handwritten letter to the United States Supreme Court, which took his case. The Court assigned Abe Fortas, the greatest lawyer of his time, as Gideon's attorney. In its landmark decision in 1963 the Court gave life to what was already in the Constitution, namely, the right to counsel as fundamental to fair trial.

In the retrial, Gideon was found not guilty after the jury deliberated just one hour. An eyewitness had lied in the first trial. *Almost 2,000 convictions in the State of Florida along were overturned as a result of Gideon v. Wainwright.* That does not mean that all the convictions were unjust, but they were achieved where the defendants were too poor to be able to afford counsel.

What the law now accords legitimacy was at one time unthinkable. Each and every legal principle that has become the bulwark of essential fairness in today's criminal law was hard-won against fierce resistance from prosecutors and the courts. As these principles gained traction over the decades, it became regrettably clear that many injustices had already occurred.

Make no mistake about defense counsel. Gideon is the pinnacle of the dogged pursuit of fairness by tireless advocates. One of society's hallmark principles is that a person's liberty should not be taken except when it is just to do so, and it cannot be just in unbalanced proceedings.

There's a wonderful twenty-minute video on You Tube about the case.

In courtrooms all across the United States, then and now, vigilant defense lawyers demand disclosure of prosecution evidence, pre-trial. They write demands for discovery and demands for bills of particulars; they ask for suppression hearings, for example, to suppress a tainted identification, or an involuntary confession illegally obtained through duress. They don't know, they aren't sure, what the prosecution has, and there are reasons that the prosecution is not required to share the evidence. In a civil trial, pre-trial disclosure is liberal, to avoid a so-called "trial by ambush". But in a criminal case there is fear that if crucial witnesses or evidence are disclosed, they might disappear before the trial. On both sides, Honor can be lost when the stakes are high.

In hard-fought cases, defense lawyers have exposed "junk science" used to convict defendants: "bite marks"; hair analysis; shaken baby syndrome; *fingerprints*, 911 call analysis.

In criminal cases there is the so-called Brady rule: the prosecution must disclose "exculpatory evidence", i.e. evidence which, if believed, would tend to *exculpate* a defendant. The prosecution is duty bound to reveal to the defense facts or evidence that is inimical to its case. Reversals of convictions are often based upon violations of this rule.

These legal principles are seen as "technicalities" by most people; until their son or daughter needs an attorney.

THE ACCIDENTALLY PERFECT SHOT

My second murder case.

Robin Fallon had entertained Billy Starr in her Hopewell home, just off Route 21. Whether there was a financial component to the evening, I never knew; but was widely suspected by the police and prosecution that Billy had not compensated Robin for her time, so to speak.

For some reason, Robin had a pistol, and as Billy left the home, the screen door hit the hand holding the pistol, and it went off. Of course, as I would assert during the trial, it was an accident as pure as the driven snow. The shooting was merely an unfortunate end of a lovely evening. That would be our theory of the case as we progressed through the trial.

But I couldn't change the fact that the shot was in Billy's back, *right through the heart!*

These were the facts of the case, set in concrete.

The unseemly subject of money was never discussed during the trial, because Billy was no longer with us, and Robin had not testified, so it could never rise above an unprovable evidentiary inference.

There was a reason Robin never testified: she left in the middle of the trial!

When she failed to appear one morning of the trial, the Judge, Hon. George Reed, asked me, "Where is your client?" I put on My Innocent Schoolboy Face and with my brow wrinkled, I said, so sincerely that it would bring tears to your eyes: "I don't know, Your Honor."

It was Ontario County Sheriff Investigator Jim McIlvene's case. He was a good cop, and a friend; used to ride with him in the wee hours. I respected him, because, while he was a tough kind of guy, he was fair, and if he gave his word to a suspect, he kept it. More than once, he went to bat with Judge Reed for an accused who had been forthright with him.

Jim found Robin in New York City the very next day! He brought her back and the trial continued.

As compelling, persuasive and, in truth, brilliant as My Lawyering was, she was found guilty. As I recall, she got fifteen years.

More than one of my So-Called Friend Lawyers would often remind me of the client who fled from me. A vote of No Confidence.

VICIOUS EVIL, PURE AND SIMPLE

As you can see from the first two cases, lawyers have a sort of black humor, devilish and perverse; it cannot be suppressed.

That was not so in my third murder case, People v. Hurley (and Green).

Howard Ringley was an RIT student. He and his wife, Gail Rhode, lived just south of the Village of Victor. A modest white ranch house on the right as you came down the hill from Boughton Hill Road.

The house is not there now, replaced by quarter million dollar homes. But I see it every time I drive down the hill.

Always will.

Mr. Ringley came home from RIT for lunch. Inside the house were my client-to-be, James Hurley, and Michael Green, who would be co-defendant. They had broken in the rear door to burglarize the place. When Mr. Ringley arrived home, they jumped him and stabbed him to death.

It was a senseless, vicious, evil, unnecessary act.

I was assigned to Hurley. A second lawyer was assigned to Green.

The prosecutor was Jim Harvey, a flamboyant trial lawyer who absolutely relished every single minute in the courtroom. He was ex-military. He used a booming voice, except when, for effect, he dropped it down to a virtual whisper, unctuous, a faint smile slyly suggesting that in a moment The Grim Reaper was coming to condemn the defendant.

Green was smart; well, cunning, like a hyena. He gave a statement in which he blamed the actual killing on Hurley, and the prosecutor went with it. Why not? Divide and conquer, as the old adage says.

One of Harvey's first witnesses, and the most powerful and poignant, was Gail Rhode. When Harvey had walked her through her grief, the other defense attorney started his cross-examination, and he continued for longer than I thought necessary. Never ask questions just for the sake of questions. Frankly, I thought it was cruel, and it was pointless.

When it was my turn, I approached somewhat, and said to her: "Ma'am, I am sorry for your loss"; and to the Judge, "Your Honor, I have no questions." I sat down.

Yes, I was sincere in wanting to spare Mrs. Rhode of more pain. But in candor, I have to add that I had learned that when a prosecution witness penetrates the jury's heart and conscience, a lawyer needs to get that witness off the stand as soon as possible.

Of course, with whatever evidence Harvey had, which I frankly do not recall now, probably forensic stuff, and certainly Green's confession, Hurley and Green were convicted. Because Green had cooperated somewhat, he got twenty-five to life. My client, Hurley: thirty-seven to life, the burglary being tacked to the murder.

There's a sequel. About a year after the trial, Gail Rhode came into my office for a will. There was no conflict of interest, because the trial was over, and I was not handling the appeal. I was humbled. She knew I had given my all in the defense, but I think she understood that the pall of sadness that overhung the trial affected everyone within the four walls of the courtroom.

It was shared sorrow.

Humanity need not be spoken. It is sometimes felt, like a warm breeze. Those of us who had walked with her in the aftermath of the cruel death of her husband were deeply affected. It was a soul-wounding case.

There's a sequel to the sequel. This lovely, elegant and dignified lady died of lupus two years later.

Tears form when I think of her now.

I will never forget her.

THE TEACHER

It was winter. February 17, 1977. My son, John was about eleven; my daughter, Suzanne, about ten. I was thirty-four, about ten years out of law school.

Can it have been forty plus years ago? Time is inexorable, like a waterfall.

Audrey Jones, a former teacher and the wife of a prominent Clifton

Springs doctor, was taking a walk in a field near the old Pearl Street Extension in the village, adjacent to where nineteen year-old James Edwards lived.

When she failed to show up for an outing with her grandchildren, a search was commenced.

Her body was found at the edge of a hedgerow. She had been shot five times -- twice in the head -- with what was determined by the police to have been a .22 caliber rifle owned by Edwards's roommate.

Footprints in the snow led from where shell casings were found to Edwards' home.

Edwards did not know Mrs. Jones. No motive was ever offered to the police at the time of the killing. It was apparently a random act committed while Edwards was rabbit hunting.

I was assigned to represent Edwards.

During the trial the prosecution introduced Edwards's written confession, and the fact that he had taken the police to the scene of the shooting and reenacted it.

Facing that evidence, I advanced a theory: because Edwards had smoked marijuana and taken LSD just prior to the murder, he was suffering from a so-called "extreme emotional disturbance." The EED defense, if successful, would drop the murder charge one notch, from intentional murder to manslaughter, which would lead to a lesser sentence. It was weak, but it was all I had.

When the proofs were closed, we had the customary "charge conference:, where the attorneys confer with the Judge, in this case, to discuss the Court's charge to the jury. The charge constitutes the Court's instructions to the jury. The usual: the presumption of innocence, which is not lost because of the introduction of *some* evidence, the requirement of proof beyond a reasonable doubt, unanimous verdict, a reading of the specific section of law alleged in the indictment, and many other principles for the jury to abide by.

I remember this as well as if it were yesterday. Near the end of the charge conference, I asked the Judge: "Is the Court going to charge the law of extreme emotional disturbance?" The Court: "Yes."

That was Friday. All weekend, I worked on my summation, which was centered on extreme emotional disturbance. No, we would not deny the killing. No, we would not deny that Edwards carried out the awful act. But he was under the influence of the marijuana and LSD, which robbed him of the ability *to form the intention* to murder Mrs. Jones; he acted under a drug-induced extreme emotional disturbance.

Monday. Court back in session. As soon as we entered the courtroom, the judge said: "Mr. Tyo, I am not going to charge extreme emotional disturbance."

I was flabbergasted, and said something like: "Your Honor, with all due respect, during the charge conference the Court indicated that it would give the charge, and my entire summation is built around it."

The judge's reply was something like: "I'll give you an hour to revise it."

I could have told myself: You wanted to be a lawyer.

James Edwards was convicted as charged and sentenced to twenty-five years-to-life.

Now, the rest of the story.

Fast forward thirty-one years. Edwards is released from prison. Seven years later he is released from parole and is living with his wife in Rochester. He wants to set the record straight, and not continue to be branded a murderer. He wants to establish his innocence of the crime and retains a lawyer to bring on a motion to vacate the conviction.

The motion is heard in Ontario County Court on June 8, 2016 by one of the sitting judges, who happens to be the son of the trial judge. (No one moved for recusal because of the kinship of the two judges.)

Edwards' attorney asserted that Edwards had always protested his innocence, but in the years since his release from prison and the pending motion, he was never able to dig up anything to establish it. But now, supposedly, he has.

The prosecution, he alleges, never told defense counsel that the shoe prints in the snow leading from the crime scene were size 7; Edwards wore size 10 1/2. Also, he claims, an eyewitness not disclosed to defense counsel saw somebody leaving the scene at about the time of the murder. That eyewitness was face-to-face with Edwards at the police station, looking at him through a two-way glass, and said he was not the person he had seen leaving the field at the time of the homicide.

This evidence, which was never revealed to me as defense counsel or the jury, counsel argued, would have exonerated his client.

The prosecution countered the motion. The written confession. The reenactment at the scene. Edwards had the opportunity to file his motion years before, but didn't. More telling, in 2008 Edwards gave an interview with a reporter from The Daily Messenger, in which he said that he did "a horrible, horrific thing", insisting he was "a changed man". He added, "I could never do what I did twenty-five years ago, today, tomorrow or ever again."

On June 22, 2017, Judge Frederick G. Reed signed an Order denying Edwards's application for vacatur of his conviction, writing that the matters raised by Edwards' attorney in the motion would not have changed the outcome of the trial, given "the overwhelming evidence against the defendant."

Had the Brady rule (disclosure of evidence favorable to the defense) been followed, had the alleged footprint and eyewitness evidence been disclosed to the prosecution, thence to me, it most certainly would have been part of my defense. Whether it might have made a difference I cannot tell. But defense counsel cannot raise what he does not know.

Of a certainty, evidence has been withheld in myriad prosecutions across the country. I will not sully the reputations of prosecutors or the police generally, but cases where evidence has been withheld give pause to any notion that the state is above chicanery.

In my career, no case proves the point more than the single most memorable criminal matter of my career.

THE KILLING OF NANCY DAVIS

Each of the many phases of this story is almost unbelievable. Many times since the years of its occurrences I have wished I had had the presence of mind to write the story as it unfolded. It was probably the press of business that kept me from doing so. After all, my assigned cases were only a part of my practice. Throughout time period these cases happened, there were literally thousands of appointments, court appearances, closings, document preparations, and the general running of a law office.

And family functions.

A major criminal case stretches over months, not days; it burns up much of one's energy; it preoccupies you; it drains you. It becomes an obsession. This was more true in no case I ever had than People v. Coleates.

There are gaps in this story, but the heart of it is here. The edges of this case are sharp enough to cut through the haze, and where the knife has become dull, I have relied on the pens of the wonderful reporters who wrote their stories about the case at the time.

A word about the free press. Without it, them, we will regress to The Dark Ages. Insidious, or worse, blatant, attacks on media, and on an independent judiciary, for that matter, are the building blocks of despots. The truth really does die in darkness. Sometimes, more recently, probably, than any time in the history of the United States, outright falsehoods are repeatedly taken in, as if by osmosis, by gullible citizens or those hostile to the truth.

To their credit, I count lawyers and the press as the most stalwart defenders of what is true.

Sorry for the digression.

The Coleates case involved about seventeen jail interviews with my client, five conferences with his father, about twenty court appearances and multiple other file contacts, such as meetings with the District Attorney and Court, contacts with doctors, my investigator, preparing memos and court orders and reviewing evidence, not to mention preparation for an unforgettable suppression hearing.

Believe it or not, I have my calendar books from those years. The entries show much of the case, but also the life around it. My son's ninth birthday; my daughter's eighth birthday, my wife's birthday, three days of fishing with my son and my friends Leo Fabris and Dick Southard and their sons at Cayuga Lake (June 23, 24 and 25, 1975), two school lunch events with my daughter, a four-day trip to Crystal City, Washington, D.C., camping on August 8, 1975 and numerous other school events.

Like a subterranean stream, People v. Coleates stealthily flowed beneath.

There were *five phases* to the case.

The *secret phase*. This never came out. It was never reported. It was my burden, and mine alone. I remember this phase as if it were yesterday.

Next, *flight*, two unbelievable coincidences: the driveby; the lawyer's office.

Then, the *suppression hearing phase*: well reported, but by far, not the whole story, not the whole truth, nothing but the truth. Part of the truth disappeared under the blue blanket of the police brotherhood.

Fourth, the *trial phase*, in which I did not participate. The second trial. The conviction and sentence.

Lastly, the *aftermath phase*, the shocking events after the conviction; and the incredible conspiracy-to-murder conviction of trial counsel, himself.

THE END OF TRANQUILITY; A DARK, HIDDEN SECRET

It is April 5, 1975, an afternoon. I am in my office in what is now our home, Liz and I. In what is now our front living room there are four secretaries. In our foyer, such as it is, a waiting room.

My office is in what is now our dining room, though in truth I never think of it as such.

There's a knock at my door. One of my secretaries tells me that there are two gentlemen in the waiting room. It is urgent that they see me.

I ask them in. They are Greg Coleates, a young man in his twenties whom I have never met, and his father, Joe.

Sitting before me, I see an agitated young man, nervous, disturbed, restless, distracted.

He blurts out: "I killed Nancy Davis".

I am stunned; but somehow, I have the presence of mind to speak to Joe immediately: "You have to leave this room right now." I know that the attorney-client privilege is compromised, broken, if there is publication of an incriminating statement to a third party.

When Joe Coleates leaves the room, I learn that Greg Coleates has been out of state in the fifteen months since Nancy Davis was stabbed to death in her mobile home on December 31st, 1973, New Year's Eve. *Over five hundred people have been interviewed* in the interim, including Greg Coleates. But no one has ever been arrested. It is an unsolved murder.

CONSCIENCE

The sense of the moral goodness or blameworthiness of one's own conduct. It is said that "a guilty conscience needs no accuser". It is a feeling of guilt and remorse so strong that it will prompt a confession where none is demanded. It is a battlefield. It is the mark of Cain, "rust on iron", a specter in the night. It is implacable and relentless.

Ultimately, it is a meltdown.

We discuss, Greg and I, whether he will turn himself in, whether he will confess, how he can, will, salve his conscience. He wants to turn himself in, with me at his side.

But first, I tell him, I need the entire story. We agree to meet at 5:00 p.m. the next day, April 6, 1975.

When he reappears, I ask whether I can tape our conversation. Yes, he says.

In the years since my practice began in 1967, we have progressed from handwriting everything, to a breadbasket-size dictaphone; and now, to a dictaphone the size of a nine-inch rectangular baking dish.

This one has four inch-wide flat elliptical tapes about seven inches long, sixteen inches in circumference. I still have the machine.

Over the next hours, Greg Coleates gives me what will fill five tapes.

We agree that I will stand with him as we contact the police. We agree to meet again, tomorrow. I give him my card.

That night, I can't sleep. Those tapes. If anything should happen to me, it is possible that they could be divulged; that the confidence could somehow be broken; that my duty to my client to preserve confidentiality could be fatally compromised.

It is probably an irrational fear. But at midnight I arise from bed and go to the office, where I shred the five tapes.

Now, only I carry this. If necessary, I know I will take it to my grave.

THE FIRST UNIMAGINABLE COINCIDENCE

Ed DeFlyer. A Shortsville resident; a friend. He is an Investigator with the Ontario County Sheriff's Office. Years later, I will form a corporation for him, Midstate Security, and he will occupy an office in what is now our bedroom.

I don't know it, but as Greg Coleates is leaving my office on the 6th, having given me the taped statement, Inv. DeFlyer *drives by the office in an unmarked investigator's vehicle.*

Coleates knows him, sees him.

An unimaginable coincidence. It will have immediate and long-range consequences.

FLIGHT

The next morning, we are in the kitchen at 14 Maple, John, Suzanne, their mother, getting ready for the day. I haven't slept well, given the midnight shred. The radio is on, and somehow it seeps into my consciousness. It is WCGR, and Russ Kimble says: "Greg Coleates has been arrested for the murder of Nancy Davis and is in the Ontario County Jail".

It strikes me like lightning. Without the slightest hesitation, breathless, I hop in the car and head to the Ontario County Jail, where I tell the jailers: "I am John Tyo. I represent Greg Coleates, I don't want anyone speaking with him. *And, I want a blood test!"*

Asking for the blood test was pure lawyer's instinct. For any of us in any walk of life, there are impulses, ready to spring like mousetraps. I knew Coleates's high was likely not natural euphoria, and drugs were a strong possibility.

PARANOIA

Later, after the suppression hearing, I learn that when Greg Coleates sees Ed DeFlyer pass by my office, he imagines that I have contacted him; that I have told him about the confession; that Ed is now on his trail. It is absurd. It is not coherent. But to Greg it is real.

After he sees DeFlyer as he leaves my office, he gets on a Greyhound bus and heads to the Adirondack region of New York State.

THE SECOND, UNTHINKABLE, COINCIDENCE

In South Glens Falls, Coleates finds his way to an attorney's office. The attorney's last name is "Tallon". This is one of the two French spellings of "Tyo"; the "lls" sound like "i" and the "n" is silent. (The other spelling is "Taille", also pronounced somewhat like "Tyo".)

The irony is surreal. We are unrelated.

In Tallon's office, Coleates goes berserk; he smashes furniture; he's screaming; he's unintelligible, he's disconnected, disjointed. Irrational. He repeats something about Nancy Davis.

Tallon calls the police, and it is relayed through the system.

A State Police Investigator is dispatched from Troop E State Police headquarters in Canandaigua, traveling to Glens Falls. There, he arrests Coleates, handcuffs him and heads back to Canandaigua, where he is taken to the Ontario County Jail.

But at the courthouse he also stops for a word with the judge's confidential secretary. He tells her, in words or effect, that Coleates was *out of his mind* during the ride from South Glens Falls to Canandaigua. Later,

I will subpoena her, the judge's personal secretary, in a hearing to try to suppress Coleates's statements and confession.

She tells the truth. But as it turns out, it doesn't matter.

BLOOD TESTS

Weeks later, the blood test I requested comes back from the lab. *Negative.*

But the DA also ordered a test. When his comes back, it is *positive*! When Greg Coleates was arrested, when he was transported from Glens Falls, when he gave his statements, he was loaded with LSD and cocaine!

Under such circumstances, can the prosecution claim Coleates's waiver of his right to remain silent, his right to counsel, was knowing, voluntary, intelligent?

NOTEBOOK; THE BLUE BLANKET

At the jail, a deputy is assigned to the hallway outside Coleates's cell. He is told to *record everything Coleates is doing*, and he does.

Coleates is crying. He is clapping. He is laughing. He is screaming. He is pacing. He is hysterical.

Somehow, from one of my police officer friends, I find out about the notebook and its contents.

But it doesn't make any difference, because when my suppression hearing is held, *the notebook is missing*!

Now, when the notebook is in Never Never Land, it is hearsay. Any mention of it is inadmissible.

It never existed.

To this day, I think I know which police officer is responsible for taking it, but I couldn't prove anything.

Lawyers are not looking through glass in their investigations; they are looking at a drab door as opaque as steel. It is evidentiary Fort Knox.

Someone in the Sheriff's Office floats the damnable lie that I took the notebook. It is nonsense: I never saw it, touched it; and if anyone wanted it in evidence, it was I.

WHAT IS SUPPRESSION?

Through the fabric of criminal law runs the thread of suppression of evidence. It is now part of the pedigree of substantive and procedural criminal law.

Evidence can be admitted into a trial if it is relevant, probative, competent and reliable.

But what if it is tainted? When the government obtains evidence in violation of an individual's constitutional rights, it will be suppressed. Such evidence is often called "fruit of the poisonous tree".

Suppression issues usually involve alleged violations of the Fourth (the prohibition against "unreasonable searches and seizures"), Fifth (right against self-incrimination) and Sixth (right to counsel) Amendments to the U.S. Constitution.

The contexts in which these issues arise are many and varied: warrantless searches of places or persons; strip searches; vehicle searches; blood tests; statements or confessions which are coerced, or taken in violation of the *Miranda* warnings, or which are the result of an illegal detention; identification issues, lineups, showups, photo arrays, composite drawings; "expert" opinion testimony, such as "repressed memory", voiceprints, hypnosis, arson investigation, handwriting, bite marks, typical features of domestic violence, abused child syndrome, child sexual abuse syndrome, bloodhounds, statistical probabilities, gang customs and rituals, accident reconstruction and blood spatter analysis. All sorts of other evidence can be the subject of suppression hearings.

Eyewitness testimony is notoriously unreliable. Hundreds of cases, hundreds of experiments, document situations where people *imagine* what they see, where two or more people see, or don't see, the same thing; or where they don't identify the same person. On top of that, there are thousands of cases where the police have *guided a witness* to an identification. One example is the so-called "six-pak". A photographic array containing six photos is handed to a witness, who is asked whether a certain perpetrator is shown. The law is replete with instances where the perpetrator is unique in the array: he is the only one with a moustache, or his skin is a different color, or he has a mark or mole, or a missing tooth, or is the only one wearing a logo hat; on and on.

Blood vials can be mis-labeled or mixed up; or the chain of custody of tangible evidence can't be established to rule out tampering. A lab can be completely discredited, as was the New York State Police Lab some years ago, where phony results were released with a straight face. (And recently, a story that DNA analyses in Colorado were manipulated for decades, affecting hundreds of convictions; the details of this report have not yet come out.)

Voodoo science. The classic example: bite mark evidence, now entirely discredited.

And confessions. Was a confession knowing, voluntary, intelligent? The challenges run the gamut. In the old days, confessions were beaten out of suspects. Suspects were held for hours without food or water, "confessing", telling the police what they wanted to hear, just to end the torment.

Extreme psychological pressure was brought to bear on suspects, such as threats that innocent family members would be charged. Requests for a lawyer were ignored. The police failed to give the warnings that the suspect has the right to silence, the right to counsel. The suspect was mentally incompetent. On and on.

Endless variations of unfair tactics exist in the taking of admissions or confessions.

The only way to counter suspect evidence, once you have a clue that it exists, it to ask the court to suppress it. Even when you don't have a clue, as a defense lawyer you have the right to ask for a hearing to explore the circumstances of the arrest and gathering of forensic evidence.

So, in such cases, a defense lawyer asks for a "suppression hearing", where the reliability of the identification or confession can be tested. If it is tainted by improper police conduct, the ID or a confession can be suppressed by the court. This means it will not allowed into evidence as part of the prosecution's case-in-chief.

THE SUPPRESSION HEARING

I brought on a motion to suppress Greg Coleates's confession that he had killed Nancy Davis. These were the grounds:

- he was so deeply under the influence of LSD and cocaine that he could not have understood his rights, much less intelligently waived them. How could he have grasped that the Fifth Amendment to the Constitution accorded him the right against self-incrimination? The Sixth Amendment Right to Counsel?
- the arresting officer admitted that he was out of his mind, i.e., not coherent;

- this was verified by the arresting officer's comment to the judge's confidential secretary;
- that a guard was assigned to monitor his conduct in his cell was proof that even the police thought there was reason to doubt his competence;
- the fact that notes were taken, but that the notebook was suspiciously lost was, itself, enough to suggest that the police did not want certain facts to come out; the hiding and withholding of this evidence was damnable and unforgivable treachery;
- and maybe, his right to counsel had "attached". He had my card in his wallet; I conceded that the right to counsel must be invoked; a suspect must announce that he wants an attorney; but it was not a spurious argument. He had already consulted with counsel, and if LSD and drugs had taken over his mind, he would not have been capable of asking for a lawyer;
- he was in a lawyer's office when he was arrested;
- Coleates's conduct in Tallon's office was far from that expected of a rational man.

The suppression hearing was epic, lasting the better part of a week. At its conclusion, the trial judge, relying on "expert opinion evidence" (forgive me, but it's a little like voodoo) given by drug experts and psychiatrists that Coleates was not so disabled by the LSD and cocaine that he could not understand, and waive, his rights, held the confession in.

To me, it was an unbelievable, though sadly not unexpected, result. The constellation of facts denigrating the reliability of my client's statements to police might as well have been in a galaxy light years away.

Sometimes lawyers feel like they are floating in space, untethered to the mother ship, unable to grasp anything tangible, unable to focus in the unreality. Of course, like the sudden stop at the end of a fatal fall, a conviction jolts defense counsel back to reality.

But if you want to insure failure, look backward. Defense lawyers, bless them, are often undeterred, like my dedicated long-time partner, Bob Zimmerman, a warrior for justice. Good lawyers know no better. They carry on the sisyphean task of defending the indefensibles.

If there's truth to the adage that adversity purifies the soul, then quite a few defense lawyers will make it through The Pearly Gates.

True. Some will head The Other Way.

NEW LAWYER, TRIALS, CONVICTION

Shortly after the suppression hearing, Greg Coleates replaced me as his attorney. He had never gotten over DeFlyer's fly-by. In Coleates's mind, DeFlyer might as well have had a sign on his vehicle: "Thanks to Tyo, I got you!"

I was unhorsed, but the case moved on, like a cattle drive.

In truth, I had done my job as assigned counsel.

After my dismissal I lost contact with the case. It's not as though I had little else to do.

But I followed news reports of the case.

Coleates hired Anthony Leonardo, one of the most prominent defense lawyers in the Rochester area. It was said that he had once gotten five consecutive not-guilty verdicts in major cases.

There were two trials. I believe that in the first trial, Greg claimed that Nancy Davis had gotten the knife, not him, maybe warded her off. Whatever. It was enough to get a hung jury.

The retrial began on April 7, 1976 and Coleates was convicted in the second trial, and sentenced to twenty-five years-to-life.

"I DID IT"

A couple years after his conviction, Coleates was the subject of a series in the Rochester Democrat and Chronicle about the case. The goal of the series was to explore whether Coleates was truly guilty of murdering Nancy Davis. As part of the series, he spoke freely to a reporter while in prison, and volunteered for a lie detector test in which he said he did not kill Nancy Davis, and didn't know who did. He failed the test.

But on April 5, 1978, in the conclusion of the series, the newspaper reported that Coleates admitted killing Nancy Davis. "I did it," he said. In a letter to his family, he apologized for all the grief he had caused.

FAST FORWARD TO 1990

An ironic twist.

In 1990 a man named Albert M. Ranieri was the inside man in an armored car heist in Henrietta, New York, which made off with $10.8 million dollars. For the next decade, he found ways to launder some of the money, sometimes using an attorney *named Anthony Leonardo*, who, along with some partners, had opened a restaurant in Charlotte. "Club Titanic" was used to cloak some of the money.

In 2000, Ranieri shot and killed Anthony Vaccaro, a local pool hall owner who was one of Leonardo's business partners. Leonardo had convinced Ranieri that Vaccaro was stealing from the club.

In 2001, Leonardo was convicted of several crimes, including conspiracy to commit murder. He admitted that he had tried to arrange the murder of Vaccaro in an execution-style ambush.

He was sentenced to Allenwood Federal Penitentiary.

For years now, every time we travel south to visit family, we pass the prison, and when I gaze right, I see Anthony Leonardo in my mind. People v. Coleates escapes from the deep memory where nothing is ever forgotten. Our mental archives are unfathomably catalogued, and, amazingly, unlike a rolodex, they are not passive; they are electronic and can be aggressive.

The Coleates case demonstrates that truth is, indeed, stranger than fiction.

HE FELL ASLEEP ON THE TOILET?

Have you ever felt foolish? I have. Many times.

One such instance involved a burglary of a well-known small restaurant on Main Street Canandaigua. I was assigned to represent an accused who was charged with burglary after he was found inside the restaurant's men's room the morning after the alleged offense.

Protesting his innocence, he told me that he had been in the restaurant during the evening, and had several drinks. When he went into the men's room, he fell asleep, and stayed asleep until the morning. (I could not bring myself to suggest to the jury how one could fall asleep on a toilet; some things are best left unexplained).

I gave my "tell all" opening to the jury, the narrative presented to me by my client. As shaky as it was, it was plausible. (I hasten to add that a trial attorney does not have to believe his clients; his job is to advocate that the client receive a fair trial).

So, blah, blah, blah, he fell asleep; there was no burglary. No harm, no foul.

Trial choreography is: the prosecutor goes first with his proof; then the defense, if it opts to present witnesses. And then the prosecutor has the opportunity for rebuttal of the defense case.

After the prosecution case, my client told his story to the jury.

Mike Tantillo, the District Attorney, one of the finest lawyers I ever met, relished his opportunity for rebuttal. Gleefully, or so it seemed to me, he called the bar owner, eliciting this depressingly effective fact: "We were not open that evening."

Using skills I learned at the Zimmerman, Tyo Lunchtime School of Acting, I maintained an air of dreamy nonchalance, even in the face of twelve very, very smug jurors, and A Smirking District Attorney.

But through very tightly gritted teeth, I leaned over to my client and quietly but firmly gave him this Very Pithy Advice: "You, sir, are going to plead guilty. Right now!"

Frankly, I do not remember the plea colloquy, but it was doubtless an occasion of great mirth for the Court and DA.

Some of my greatest, most passionate and effective speeches were made in my car on the way home. In this case, it was a short speech: "You wanted to be a lawyer."

INEFFECTIVE ASSISTANCE OF COUNSEL

I was assigned to the appeal of a lady named "Pam". She had been convicted of larceny in Ontario County Court.

On the facts and on the law, she was guilty.

But every criminal accused has a right to an appeal, provided a Notice of Appeal is timely filed. Appeals from Ontario County Court are made to the Appellate Division, Fourth Department, located on East Avenue in Rochester. The appeals are heard by its five-judge panel.

With Liz's help in organizing, printing and assembling the documents necessary to an appeal, we filed over 300 appeals over the years, most to the Appellate Division, Fourth Department, and while appeals are often "submitted" to the court without an appearance before the five-judge panel,

I often appeared, even if my arguments were short and to the point. And with regularity, hopeless. Even when the appeal was hopeless, the justices on the court were very courteous. I always had the greatest respect for them. If they had any for me, it may have been because in my briefs, I was *always* true to the facts in the record. It is so easy to embellish the facts, but it is dishonest, and the justices will find it. The Appellate Division Fourth Department was known as a "hot" court, meaning that they had read the record and briefs prior to the oral argument, not always the case in other courts.

There are two major parts to an appeal: the Record on Appeal and the Brief.

Counsel for an appellant must order the Record, which consists of the Indictment, all the defense discovery motions and the People's responses to the same, the transcripts of every court appearance, including any trial, and the pre-sentence report. These are all set forth in a particular order as outlined in the Table of Contents.

Once the Record on Appeal is ready, counsel can prepare the Brief, which itself has certain parts set forth in a particular order: an brief overview of the nature of the appeal, including a summary statement listing the court, the charges, the name of the presiding judge, the names of counsel and a statement of the convictions appealed from.

Next, a Statement of Facts, mentioned above.

Finally, the Points of the Brief, which are the legal arguments sought to provide the basis for a reversal of the conviction.

After the Record on Appeal and Briefs are submitted to the Court in the required number of copies, the Court schedules a date for oral argument. Counsel then has the option to "submit on the papers" or to appear.

In this case, as is mentioned above, there was no doubt about Pam's guilt.

But on this appeal my brief asserted that she had been denied the effective assistance of counsel.

Pam had retained an attorney at the trial level of the case, who I will call "Jason". His representation was classically incompetent. He missed court appearances, or was late in appearing. He failed to file appropriate pre-trial motions. He made utterly unbelievable excuses for his lapses and omissions. He turned the trial in to a farce, his legal assertions garbled and confused, his trial strategy inept, disorderly and ill conceived. On several occasions he infuriated the judge and received pointed rebukes from him.

Pam finally exercised the single option left open to her: she entered a guilty plea.

In the appeal, I argued that Pam's conviction was unjust because she was deprived of the effective assistance of counsel, based upon the principals established by the United States Supreme Court in the landmark case, *Gideon vs. Wainwright,* mentioned above, the facts of which are stated in the Court's opinion, and briefly mentioned above.

"Clarence Earl Gideon was an unlikely hero. He was a man with an eighthgrade education who ran away from home when he was in middle school. He spent much of his early adult life as a drifter, spending time in and out of prisons for nonviolent crimes.

Gideon was charged with breaking and entering with the intent to commit a misdemeanor, which is a felony under Florida law. At trial, Gideon appeared in court without an attorney. In open court, he asked the judge to appoint counsel for him because he could not afford an attorney. The trial judge denied Gideon's request because Florida law only permitted appointment of counsel for poor defendants charged with capital offenses.

At trial, Gideon represented himself he made an opening statement to the jury, crossexamined the prosecution's witnesses, presented witnesses in his own defense, declined to testify himself, and made arguments emphasizing his innocence. Despite his efforts, the jury found Gideon guilty and he was sentenced to five years imprisonment.

Gideon sought relief from his conviction by filing a petition for writ of habeas corpus in the Florida Supreme Court. In his petition, Gideon challenged his conviction and sentence on the ground that the trial judge's refusal to appoint counsel violated Gideon's constitutional rights. The Florida Supreme Court denied Gideon's petition.

Gideon next filed a *handwritten* petition in the Supreme Court of the United States. The Court agreed to hear the case to resolve the question of whether the right to counsel guaranteed under the Sixth Amendment of the Constitution applies to defendants in state court."

Abe Fortas, one of the ablest lawyers in the land and future Supreme Court Justice, agreed to represent Gideon without fee.

On March 18, 1963, the United States Supreme Court announced that people accused of crimes have a right to an attorney even if they cannot afford one. That seminal case revolutionized criminal law throughout the United States. It was also the basis for reversals of several hundred Florida convictions.

At his retrial, Gideon was found not guilty."

My appeal on behalf of Pam received a warm welcome from the Justices of the Appellate Division, Fourth Department, which reversed her conviction. Any appellate counsel could have achieved the same result with the compelling facts of the case. In fact, the District Attorney candidly agreed with the defendant that she was denied the effective assistance of counsel.

The Court's decision summarized Pam's plight:

"Viewing the evidence, the law and the circumstances of these cases in totality we agree with defendant and the People that she was denied meaningful representation (see People v. Baldi, 54 N.Y.2d 137, 147). From the inception of his representation of defendant in these matters, defense counsel made clear that defendant's cases were not a priority for him. Prior to trial on the charges in the first indictment (appeal No. 1), he filed no motions on her behalf with respect to the charges in either indictment and consistently requested adjournments due to other allegedly more important matters. Moreover, he was ill-prepared at the hearings that he did attend and demonstrated an utter lack of proficiency in criminal law matters. The conduct of defense counsel during the trial on the charges in the first indictment (appeal No. 1) reflected his total lack of preparation and, indeed, he called a witness whose testimony undercut his defense strategy. Finally, at the end of the second day of trial, he admitted that he had been "trying to get out of this as quick as I could for as long as I [could]." Defendant requested substitution of counsel based on her attorney's poor performance, and County Court denied her request. Defendant then pleaded guilty under the two indictments and waived her right to appeal. Because defendant's pleas were infected by ineffective assistance of counsel (cf. People v Petgen, 55 N.Y.2d 529, 535, rearg denied 57 N.Y.2d 674) and defendant entered the pleas because of her attorney's poor performance, we reverse the judgments, vacate defendant's pleas of guilty and remit the matters to Ontario County Court for further proceedings on the indictments. People v. Laraby, 305 A.D.2d 1121, 1122 (N.Y. App. Div. 2003)

Though she received no assistance from her trial attorney, she retained her composure throughout. And when she returned to Ontario County Court after the convictions were reversed, she entered guilty pleas. When she did that, she thanked the Court for the opportunity to reappear; she told the Court that the criminal justice system had treated her well, and that she was appreciative that it allowed her to finalize her two crimes in a fair manner. She was humble and contrite.

Her lawyer had failed her, but the legal system had not.

FIDEL CASTRO'S AMBASSADORS

I include this case in this narrative only to show that defense counsel can take no part of a prosecution case for granted; he cannot be credulous, even at the expense of challenges that verge on the ridiculous. And sometimes, near comedy.

In short, if you don't ask questions you won't learn any facts, and sometimes the questions seem ridiculous because they come from the dark shadows of the case.

Somewhere around the early 1980's I was assigned to a man who had come to the United States from Cuba with the permission of Fidel Castro. One can read about the so-called Mariel Boatlift today, but I was completely unaware of the contextual facts at the time. I am aware now that many Cubans wanted to flee Cuba. Thousands of asylum seekers flocked to embassies in Havana. Castro called them "bums, antisocial elements, delinquents, and trash." Among those allowed by Castro to leave were some, as I now read in Wikipedia, undesirables, criminals and mental patients. The United States agreed to accept a certain number of those fleeing Cuba. I hasten to add that most were genuinely good people seeking a better life. There were a few whom Castro foisted off on American good will.

All this background was unknown to me, and, in any event, irrelevant. All I knew was that I had been assigned to one of the refugees.

I do not remember his name. In fact, I do not remember the outcome of his case, though we all can guess what it was.

What I do remember is that the facts of the case are....... how shall I put it?.......... somewhat indelicate.

The facts were adduced at a so-called *probable cause hearing*, the request for which was contained in my *omnibus motions*. After an accused is arraigned on charges, defense counsel has forty-five days in which to prepare motions: discovery, bill of particulars about the alleged crime; suppression of wrongfully-obtained evidence, etc. One part of those motions can be a claim by the defense that there was no probable cause to arrest the defendant. The Fourth Amendment to the United States Constitution requires that police have probable cause to believe that a crime has been or is being committed before they make an arrest, obtain a warrant or conduct a search.

One must understand, as I have mentioned elsewhere, defense counsel is not given a storybook by the prosecution; much of his knowledge comes from his client, who, unfortunately is not always reliable, and from what he can pry from the cold-handed clutches of the DA. The defense motions are an attempt to ascertain vital information, to assess the strength of the prosecution's case. Even then, much of the People's case can come as a surprise at trial.

In any event, at the hearing I requested, the prosecutor called two young girls. As I recall it, they were walking on the sidewalk in the business district of Geneva when a pearl-handled revolver came flying through the glass of a second-floor window, falling on the sidewalk. The girls were quick-thinking. They agreed that one would step in to a doorway to direct the police and the other would go to the police station.

When a police officer arrived he went up the stairs, where behind the opening door was a young female and my client. His pants were around his ankles and he had .... well, I guess we are all adults here....... an erection.

Now I can still see Jack Smith, the court clerk at the time, a wonderful and perceptive guy, almost losing it when I asked the officer: "Officer, you stated that my client had an erection. Are we talking ninety degrees?"

The officer: "No. More like one hundred and ten."

With that answer my attempt to dispute the officer's testimony went down the drain, somewhat hilariously. Again, I thought to myself, for the hundredth time, you wanted to be a lawyer.

I do have one other recollection of the case. My client was Spanish-speaking; he knew no English. The court had to bring in an interpreter.

Now, the prosecutor was none other than James R. Harvey, who relished every single cross-examination he ever had. It's an exaggeration, true, but I could almost see him quivering, like a pre-jump cat, as he waited for his chance. And he knew theater. In one series of questions he might speak in a normal voice while nodding his head in a form of sardonic and insincere agreement. And then, he might suddenly follow his unspoken sarcasm with thunderous armor-piercing questions, many of which sounded a lot like accusations.

A defense lawyer can warn a witness about his own demeanor, how to be respectful, how not to argue with the other lawyer, etc. But once he takes the stand, he has to expect an energetic cross-examination.

To my delight, however, Harvey's questions had to be directed to the *interpreter*, who had, in truth, done no wrong. And a Harvey question that started out as a blast of frigid wind wound up as a warm breeze as it reached my client. Also, the cadence of Harvey's cross-examination, which started out as military march, wound up as a stroll through a flower garden.

It is pathetic, the small victories defense counsel can savor as salvage from utter devastation.

I'm sure that in the end justice was served, because I am quite certain that my client is not one whom I "got off".

THE TAIL OF THE WHALE

I don't recall the dates, but in the mix with the cases mentioned above, I was assigned to defend Anthony Oliveri.

He was "connected", so to say.

In one of the outbuildings at East View Mall there was a restaurant called "Tail of the Whale". Someone had burglarized it, opened a floor safe behind the bar, and stolen the money in the safe.

I distinctly recall several visits with Oliveri at the Ontario County Jail. I would ask him what happened, what he knew about the theft.

Oliveri was a seasoned felon; he was cagey, canny, like a fox. He would always say, "Now, you gotta understand, I wasn't there. But if I was there, this is what would have happened."

And in his transparent hypothetical way, he told me that the theft was an inside job. Someone had left the door ajar, and had spun the necessary numbers on the safe combination to allow access.

In trial, the prosecution called witnesses to relate details about the restaurant, the physical setting, where the safe was, who worked there, how much was taken, etc.

The last witness was one of the employees, called to verify some of those details.

My turn.

There is an unspoken tenet of trial lawyers: *never ask a question to which you do not already know the answer*! If you get an answer that kills you, you cannot "unring the bell", as lawyers say. You asked for it; you got it.

I wasn't sure what the witness would say.

But I took a breath. "Did someone leave the door ajar?"

"Yes."

"Did someone run the combination of the safe, so it was able to be opened?"

"Yes."

Here goes: *"Do you know who that was?"*

"Yes, but it wasn't anyone in this courtooom."

It was one of those rare moments where a trial lawyer wants to shout "Hallelujah!!!" Bells go off; fireworks light the sky. But he or she must maintain that air of stoicism. Nonchalance. Yes, of course, that's what we thought. As close to smugness as you can get. But don't show it to the jury.

Which acquitted Oliveri.

During the trial, my Dad, retired from 35 years as a Rochester Transit bus driver, sat in the gallery. The police thought he was going to be a surprise witness. They kept checking him out. I let them stew.

Finally, one of them asked me who was the gentleman sitting throughout the trial. I told him, "Oh, that's my Dad." Only I saw Dad's smirk.

I still see it.

After the verdict, he and I went to lunch at "Charlie's Restaurant", a little way down Main Street, Canandaigua.

A man came over, dressed in a sport coat, his shirt collar splayed outside. Gold chain around his neck. He was all exaggerated hand gestures, smiling, hunching his shoulders. Big nose. Brooklyn accent. Took me about three seconds to figure out that he was one of Oliveri's "connections".

"Ay, 'ow you doin'? Nice job inere. Anyting you need. Lemme buyyou lunch. Maybe we can sen you some business..."

I told him, no, I'm having lunch with my Dad, and I'm paying for it. And I don't need any business.

The last thing I wanted or needed was to become a small-time consiglieri, owned, obligated.

I would happily return to my life of quiet obscurity.

MISCELLANEOUS ODDS 'N ENDS

UM..... IS THAT A JETLINER?

In the late 1960s and early 1970s the Villages of Shortsville and Manchester were trying to relieve the economic and housing strangle caused by the lack of adequate sewerage facilities. Each village had a treatment facility, but each facility was outdated and ill equipped to serve the villages into the future. That fact had an impact upon construction of new homes.

The villages hired engineers to design a single sewage treatment facility and connecting lines, and to help shepherd the project through the Department of Environmental Conservation.

I represented both villages. We were set to move forward with the project.

But the first attempt failed when then President Richard Nixon impounded the government funds necessary to finance the project. According to Wikipedia, impoundment was an act by a President of the United States of not spending money *that had been appropriated by the U.S. Congress.* Thomas Jefferson was the first president to exercise the power of impoundment in 1801. The power was available to all presidents up to and including Richard Nixon, and was regarded as a power inherent to the office, although one with limits. The Congressional Budget and Impoundment Control Act of 1974 was passed in response to perceived abuse of the power under President Nixon. The Act removed that power.

In time, the villages revived the project, which would be financed with so-called bond anticipation notes (BANs) during construction and municipal bonds for the permanent financing

I prepared the legal documents, starting with a so-called intermunicipal agreement permitted under the New York State General Municipal Law. Bond counsel prepared the BANS and municipal bonds.

We had several meetings with the DEC in Albany. Our engineer, Wayne Ackert of Lozier Engineers in Rochester, arranged for us to fly to one of those meetings. We took off in a small plane from what I liked to call Williamson-Sodus International Airport. When we landed in Albany our pilot said he would wait at the airport until we returned.

After the meeting we returned to the airport and boarded the plane.

Um.... was that a wee bit of an alcoholic beverage I smelled?

The pilot proceeded down the taxiway, then turned right, heading toward the runway.

Looking to my left, um... was that a passenger airliner nearing a landing *on our intended runway*?

Sitting behind the pilot, I grabbed his shoulder and said "Wait!"

At the same time I heard air control say "I told you to stop at the end of the taxiway!"

Avoiding what would have been a serious "incident" the pilot stopped before we entered the runway, and managed to get us back to Williamson-Sodus International Airport.

We never again flew to Albany. The so-called STP (Sewage Treatment Plant) was built and is still in service today.

As is true with so many legal matters, it is a small step from The Mundane to The Thrilling.

MAYBE IT'S NOT SO BAD IN SIBERIA

Have you ever cracked a joke you thought was hilarious? But no one laughed?

It was around 1970, my first year practicing in Canandaigua after three years in Rochester.

The bar was invited to a cocktail party at the close of business at the main office of Canandaigua National Bank on Main Street, Canandaigua.

I decided to go, and upon my arrival I saw a number of attorneys clustered around the "bar". It was literally *a card table* on which there was a container of ice cubes, some paper cups and *one* bottle of some kind of whiskey.

To say that it was parsimonious would be to exaggerate it.

After a few minutes, a young bank associate introduced the bank president who was the epitome of austerity. Tall, thin, ramrod straight with a humorless countenance, he spoke glowingly about the bank's success and lofty position in the world of banking. I'm sure I do not remember the remarks, except to say that one part of the short presentation was that the bank could support all our needs while containing costs. It was in a very strong competitive position, said the president.

At the conclusion of the president's remarks, the young banker stepped in, ostensibly to conclude the presentation. He thanked the bank president for his remarks and then, to us, he said, with a cheerful smile: "I can tell you why the bank is so successful. *They don't pay their employees very well.*"

The hushed silence that followed was similar to what one might find listening to a eulogy.

The young man's attempt at levity was a catastrophic failure. The lawyers knew the bank president and when the remark was made saw his stern unsmiling look. He made no attempt to rescue the young man.

All that was missing was an orchestra playing a funeral dirge.

I could have made the event complete with a loud guffaw; but Providence must have been watching over me and, taking my clue from the older lawyers, I stifled my thin smile.

Last I knew, the young banker was a clerk in a small bank in Siberia.

THE LAWSUIT I COULDN'T AFFORD

Tax abatement.

Two of the dirtiest words in the lexicon of legal affairs.

It is corporate welfare played out by cowering municipalities worried that economic development will migrate to another cowering municipality. They are rivals, like those birds with the crazy antics trying to attract a mate.

It's the lawsuit I wanted to bring, but couldn't afford.

Imagine a small city, like, say, Canandaigua, New York.

Imagine that it rests at the head of one of the beautiful so-called Finger Lakes.

Imagine that right at the northern tip of the lake there's a hotel assessed at nine million dollars.

Imagine that a *for profit* corporation, I'll call it "FPC" decides to tear the hotel down and build a new hotel and conference center valued at, say, forty million.

Imagine a so-called "Economic Development Agency" (EDA), and imagine that it is autonomous. That is, no taxing entity, not the county, not the city, not the town, not the school district, has any authority over it. Once created by the County Board of Supervisors its actions, what I'll call "powers to gift" are beyond the control of any entity supported by taxpayers. Oh, the county board of supervisors could disband the EDA, but instead, it embraces it like a lover.

Also imagine that the EDA is authorized by a 1969 statute. It has the appearance of a creature of state because it is created by the state but it has the power to give state money to private entities, *circumventing the gift and loan provision of the New York State Constitution.*

Now imagine that FPC approaches EDA and says: "Gee, we'd like to build our palatial hotel and conference center, but the taxes would be too much. If we could get some *tax abatement*, we would build it. They submit a study to a gullible EDC board which study glibly claims that the location of the new hotel will remedy an economically depressed zone, when residential property around Canandaigua Lake is among the most expensive in the U.S.

Cut to the chase: here's what happened:

- FPC tore down the existing hotel;
- the resulting vacant lot was reassessed to about half of its former value;
- the EDA granted FPC's application for tax abatement for the new hotel, agreeing to tax the project at $4.6 million, down from the $40 million projected value of the project on completion;
- the tax abatement would be in effect for *ten years.*

I came close to flunking fourth grade math, but I retained enough to know that $4.6 million is about 10% of the $40 million of the value of the completed project. Conversely, 90% is tax free for the next ten years.

Not in this case specifically, but in a 2011 case, *Bordeleau vs. New York*, the New York Court of Appeals ruled that the Constitution "permits the granting of public funds to public benefit corporations *for a public purpose*" (emphasis added). Turning to a second question, whether or not the recipient of the funds, i.e., the EDA, could *turn them over* to a *private organization* for the promotion of New York agricultural products (apples and grapes), the Court found "no constitutional infirmity" because the funding was "for the overall benefit of the public and the State's competitiveness."

My question was, and is: how does throwing taxpayer dollars at a for-profit corporation benefit the public?

This is the lawsuit I desperately wanted to bring. I would ask for a declaratory judgment that tax abatement is an illegal government gift, and I would request an injunction interdicting the grant of tax abatement. I would seek to re-argue *Bordeleau* on the specific facts of this case, and would cite Court of Appeals Justice Eugene Piggott's dissent: "that the defendants' arguments 'are precisely the kind of claims that sully taxpayers' view of our state government.'" He pointed out that there is no fundamental difference between the State directly giving monies to *private enterprises* and the State creating *public corporations* with the express intent of doing so.

Justice Smith agreed, authoring this pithy sentence: "It is an illusion - one that seems to have the persistence of original sin - that prosperity can be attained by taking money from taxpayers and handing it to favored businesses." His dissent expressed frustration and annoyance that the State can commit the precise folly the Constitution was designed to prevent.

I spent many hours of impotent rage in the service of what was My Pet Peeve at the time (I have others now.) I obtained copies of the so-called supporting documents submitted by FPC to EDA, organized them, marshaled my arguments, wrote letters to the editor and attended the meeting where the discussion was immediately followed by a vote favoring the abatement.

But caution is a necessary counterpart to rage.

How could I fight a one-man war? In time, in money, how could I find a way to enlist public moral support and/or volunteer attorneys? public financial support? pay for filing fees? document preparation with multiple copies of voluminous materials? call on our law firm staff to help assemble and copy thousands of pages of documents? hire experts to debunk the voodoo financial assertions of both FPC and EDA? appear at motions and trial, and, possibly, afford an appeal?

It wasn't feasible, especially if I were trying to wage a battle while still attending to a private law practice.

A colorful Ontario County Judge was fond of using the term, "Mushbrains." That would be my friends and I, and my clients, shouldering our fair share of our real property tax bills, but not being able....... oh, did I forget to say that we need to be a guest of The New Palace I'll call it, to have lakefront access?

No little urchins will dip their dirty toes in the waters sloshing up against the concrete retaining wall at The New Palace.

I say, bluntly: *disband all of the EDAs in New York State and let business sink or swim on its merits, like the rest of us; or move to another state where the grass is greener.* Until it isn't.

SAFETY HARNESSES IN THE SHOWERS?

My neighbor and long-time friend, Leo Fabris, could have been a brilliant lawyer; no question about it. Instead, he became one of the finest and most-loved teachers Redjacket Central ever had, or ever will have. Social studies. A fierce advocate for young minds.

We met in our backyards back in 1969, soon after our purchase of 14 Maple Avenue. In our conversation we learned that we were both raised in Rochester. At some point I mentioned that my grandfather, Bert Smith, had emigrated from England, settling in Rochester. I also mentioned that he had been the chief baker at The Powers Hotel back in its heyday. At that,

Leo exclaimed: "Smitty?!" He had worked with him when he was a young man!

Small world, as they say.

Anyway, one day Leo told me he was going to be away for three days, and asked me whether I might like to substitute teach for him.

I jumped at the chance. I had a degree in history with a minor in English and was qualified to teach. Well, on paper. I had little real classroom experience with students.

Now, I was much more conservative back then in the 1980's than I am now. And in Leo's Regents Social Studies class, discussing whether or not government was too intrusive and too paternalistic, I happened to mention, **in jest**, that New York was considering a law which would require that we install *safety harnesses in our showers*. For our own protection, of course, which, as usual, would justify the intrusion. I thought my exaggeration was a good way to make a point.

But wouldn't you know it? Several of the students wrote it as a fact in their Regents exams.

Later, after he had heard from the Regents examiners, Leo asked me: "What the heck did you tell them about safety harnesses in the showers??"

I sheepishly admitted that I had said it, but was joking!

In retrospect, I gather that the students did not know me well enough to recognize my attempt at humor for what it was.

And I must say that those three days of teaching were exhausting. It was like putting on a one-man play three times a day for three days.

I went back to law, where I belonged, but with immensely heightened respect for the teaching profession.

GLIMPSES OF A COUNTRY LAW OFFICE

This is truly mundane, but if one wants a look into a country law office, this may be helpful.

To begin with, elsewhere in this book we have seen that practicing law is not a money-making business; it is more than that. However, there are obvious financial components in making a living in any employment position, and law is no exception.

If one Googles average lawyer salaries, one will find all sorts of studies with all sorts of results. Zip Recruiter presents a fair distillation or comparison of the various studies, suggesting New York lawyer salaries as high as $150,976 and as low as $51,420. The majority of lawyer salaries currently range between $86,400 (25th percentile) to $112,700 (75th percentile) with top earners (90th percentile) making $143,318 annually in New York. (How, if at all, the negligence lawyers who tout long lists of million dollar verdicts skew the figures I have no idea, but the figures for "salaries as high as...." are certainly anemic. I have to believe that the average earnings cited above are for lawyers in the trenches, as I like to call them: um, us.)

How the lawyer practices and in what fields does he choose to practice make a significant impact on his or her earnings.

Examples:

a. A solo lawyer with one or two paralegals;
b. A solo lawyer with *no staff*.
c. A law partnership or PC with two or more lawyers and corresponding staff.

In Ontario and surrounding counties there are a few lawyers who have a solo practice and *no staff*. For instance, a lawyer in Canandaigua has practiced for decades doing solely real estate. He does all the document preparation, attends the closings, handles the lenders, does the closeout, disburses the funds.... all without the assistance of a secretary/paralegal. Did I mention that he *keeps* all the fees his practice generates? Not that I recommend such a lonely practice.

The lack of an employee means minimal expenses. That is, he has no employee payroll; no federal or state payroll taxes; no Workers Comp insurance; no disability insurance; no unemployment insurance; and no reporting to any of those entities. But he misses all the fun of having paralegals, and the ability to take on all sorts of non-real estate matters.

A solo lawyer with one or two paralegals has the advantage of their assistance in a multitude of office duties, better coverage of the office hours, better phone coverage, two or three minds rather than one in solving problems, and endlessly helpful detailed document preparation; and of course, the ability to diversify in the kinds of matters undertaken.

Zimmerman & Tyo is the third alternative: the law partnership with two or more lawyers and corresponding staff.

Prior to the start of the Zimmerman & Tyo partnership in 1985, I had relatively short-term associates, namely Jim Miller, Esq. and Jack Schuppenhauer, Esq. After a year or two, they started their own practices.

At Z&T we served a wide variety of clients. Bob was almost exclusively criminal, while I handled wills, estates, real estate, matrimonials, family court, general business contracts, two municipalities, some criminal and several hundred criminal appeals. Our work loads were equivalent.

We never had less than three paralegals, and for a time, four.

When our modest income stream was consistent, we were able to make a decent living, each earning something between the high and low average lawyer salaries mentioned above.

I hasten to add that it was *always* a struggle; making payroll and all the government withholding, required employee insurances and reporting; $12,000 annual library expense, $6,000 malpractice insurance, $18,000 annual rent, plus postage, supplies, etc.; our overhead was close to overwhelming. But we never let any of our paralegals go; we were always able to cover their modest salaries. And they gave us the advantage of vast institutional knowledge and the ability to provide legal services to the community in all sorts of client matters.

But in economic downturns, of which there were several, we were often on the brink. I will never forget two things about this: First, there were a few times when my wife, Liz, our bookkeeper (and paralegal) and I could be on opposite sides of a crowded room and see the fear in each other's eyes. How were we ever going to cover all the expenses while at the same time keeping up our estimated tax payments to Uncle Sam and New York state?

Second, one payday our basic payroll was $2,300 for one week; we had total liquid assets of $2,000. For one week I drove to a little luncheonette in Palmyra where no one would know me, and took the books with me. Then Bob and Liz and I figured out a plan to put some cost-saving measures in place; we cut a few hours off the payroll; we slimmed down our draws somewhat; we prioritized what obligations we would pay first; we took a closer look at our fee structures, which were always on the low end; increasing the fees was overdue, and it was the key to our survival, even if they were nevertheless modest by comparison with others.

We weathered the storm, one of many over our 37 year partnership.

Along the way we were able to maintain certain virtues:

We never advertised. Both Bob and I were taught in law school that lawyers are passive in that they should receive clients who have sought them out, rather than seeking them out with self-promotional ads and sound bytes;

- We grew with the demand, providing legal services to an increasingly wide-spread clientele;
- We never did car crashes; a few times when clients came in with such matters, we referred them out. You can't avoid the TV commercials; Hurt in a Car? That's where the money is for lawyers. But it is a specialty, with rigid unforgiving time limitations, endless discovery, possible trial preparation; it would have been too demanding for Z&T, and would have precluded our giving assistance to our clients in many other matters. I hasten to add that litigation is an

incubator for paranoia. It is exacting and unforgiving, and if you do not specialize in it, you will regret it.
- While we stayed busy, we avoided a factory-like atmosphere, such as many offices face in representing demanding real estate lenders; we tried to balance how many matters could we and our staff handle. And our staff covered for each other so that there was never a time when family was neglected.
- We took the bad with the good; in other words, we did not cherry pick the matters we would take. I often told myself jokingly that we would take a dog barking case that the big-fee-billable hours lawyers wouldn't dream of taking; but if your broke your neck in a car crash they would hug your ankles to get you in their office.
- We kept our fees reasonable. For example, many lawyers charged an up-front retainer of anywhere between $3,500 and $10,000 for a divorce. Ours was $1,500, and there were many times when we waited for our fees until the clients could afford to pay us. The same with Bob's criminal cases and the same with estates.

A related factor: we sold The Parlour Village Office Building to the Village of Shortsville. We did not make a lot of money on the sale, but we were able to gain relief from expenses, such as mortgage payments, insurance and real property taxes.

If I were to look backward, my focus would not be on the financial ups and downs of our practice; rather it is on what I call "the loveable mundane" of helping good folks with their legal problems.

`Speaking of mundane, aside from strictly legal and/or financial issues, the country law office offered training in many other skills: taking out the trash and recycling; vacuuming the entire office, ordering supplies, cleaning the bathrooms, dealing with suppliers, managing files and purging them every five years or so; just to name a few.

Lest I forget: the key to our practice was our secretaries/paralegals. I make no distinction between them: if you work in a law office, you are a paralegal, because every single day you will be called upon to deal with some kind of problem. You do not need a paralegal degree to be effective and competent. Beginning in 1967 with my three and a half years with Remington, Gifford, Wiley & Williams, as previously mentioned I was fortunate to work with at least twenty-two paralegals. From among them I am especially indebted to five: Lucille Dobbler, Barb Berdzinski, Teri Gersbach, Janice Shannon and Liz Tyo. They are each in the central core of my career; each a vital part of it; the standard bearers of our institutional integrity, our professionalism and our commitment to our community.

TREASURES OTHER THAN GOLD

Those are what are to be found in a rural setting.

My friend, Dick Southard, gone these many years, had a favorite Bible passage: "To whom much is given, much is asked."

All attorneys are taught in law school that they have a professional responsibility, an ethical obligation, to provide legal services to individuals who cannot afford an attorney. Such a moral ideal is a repudiation of one of Shakespeare's villains, Dick the Butcher, who utters the famous quote: "The first thing we do is, let's kill all the lawyers."

Olivia Rutigliano in *Lit Hub*, explains the quote: "Then as now lawyers were more available to the wealthy and powerful, who could afford to retain them, than to the poor and the weak, and were the very symbols of the inequities and oppression that provoke a revolution. As a result, the folk image of lawyers has often been bad. Common people have frequently seen lawyers in their roles as conservative defenders of property and the status quo, as unethical 'hired guns' or 'mouthpieces' available to the highest bidder, as a professional elite of technical wizards adept at using the law to cheat honest but poor people. Many upright citizens, wearied by what Hamlet called 'the law's delay' or caught in the intricacies of legal red tape, must have bitterly' echoed Dick the Butcher's sentiment through clenched teeth at one time or another."

Forgive me, but there is no better example of these sentiments than certain lawyers (and lawmakers who are lawyers) in the Trump years, most of whom are still practicing despite their patently unethical, dishonest, unfounded, baseless damnable filings. These outliers without virtue exemplify how societal and governmental values can casually be discarded in the pursuit of power. They have forgotten, or never appreciated, their favored status in life and the obligations that go with it.

But no; if you would seek a balanced view of the profession, look to the thousands of lawyers who champion the less privileged and who contribute something of value to the communities in which they live.

I learned the value of public service first and foremost from my law partner, Bob Zimmerman, who always and steadfastly committed his time and energy to worthwhile causes.

Taking a cue from Bob Zimmerman, I served two six-year stints on the 7th Judicial District Grievance Panel, the disciplinary arm of the New York State Appellate Division, which oversees lawyer conduct.

I served six years on the Board of Legal Assistance of Western New York, a not-for-profit group of, for lack of a better description, poverty lawyers; in other words, legal services for the poor. A wonderful organization serving eight Western New York counties. I served as president of the board for three of the six years. Again, I followed Bob Zimmerman.

I served six years as Board member, three as Board president, for Finger Lakes Area Counseling and Recovery Agency; again, a wonderful organization. Its counselors provided tough love, but without judgment, a virtue easily beyond my reach until my association with the organization. Another instance of following Bob's service.

Finally, Bob and I leap-frogged each other as Presidents of the Ontario County Bar Association.

I also served three years as Chair of the Ontario County Republican Party. That was back in the mid-1980s, when that party had integrity. Meaning, it was before Rush Limbaugh's phony "Excellence In Broadcasting Network" and red MAGA hats.

And so, along the way, I found myself active in community affairs. I mention these not as a matter of pride, but to add to the narrative country lawyers' immersion in the community, and the opportunities to add value to lives.

I also served two three-year terms on the New York State Bar Association House of Delegates, the decision and policy-making body of the Association.

One lawyer summed it up with a single quote from a longtime client near the end of his practice: "We will miss you; you have been a resource for this community."

Whether the age of high-tech specialization and the internet will eliminate country lawyers, who are generalists, is yet to be seen. Like the country doctors who made house calls, country lawyers are somewhat a throwback to what now seems a kinder age.

But those of us who still hear the calling will doubtless opt not for the driverless auto, but for the next stagecoach, to carry us on our rounds.

CONFIDATIONS TO A COUNTRY LAWYER

CLIENT MALAPROPS LOVINGLY COLLECTED OVER THE DECADES

The following is a collection of over fifty years' worth of memorable, and loveable, statements made to a country lawyer, who has saved them with the same affection he possesses for the clients, and with the knowledge that Providence has graced even serious situations with Humor.

MEDICINE

1. "Why didn't they talk to me face to face? Check my complexion, to see if I was lying."
2. "I need to get a power of attorney from my father, but he's inconfident."
3. "I woke up in the hospital. They told me, 'George, you're in Buffalo, and you've got one more hour in the air-conditioning machine.'"
4. "This has been a trimatic experience."
5. "I don't know what's wrong with him. But I know he didn't take his ejection this morning."
6. "They were supposed to give her a shot, right in the beginning."

7. "I've got to re-do my will. I'm so upset. My sister just got out of instant care."
8. "He had a disease. But it's not maligament."
9. "Somebody told me she had a veneral disease."
10. "I'm transferring her to extensive care."
11. "Maybe they can do less evasive surgery."
12. "I ordered new shoes. They give me good gription."
13. "She been in the physic ward three times."
14. "My wife has been diagnosed as a maniac-depressive."
15. "I couldn't say. I don't remember. I was in the hospital, and I was heavily seduced."
16. "The problem is, he's got undiminished capacity."
17. "I had a mammogram on my back."

POSSIBLE LITIGATION

1. "I'd sue him. I'd have no quim about it."
2. "I'm not degruding the guy anything, but I'm not giving him a cent."
3. "I want to sue him for eleven hundred thousand dollars."
4. "I want you to sue him for $20,000 for deprivation of character."
5. "I didn't tell her to move to Hillside Apartments. But she's already had three conviction notices."
6. "I hit him one and he did a somerset beneath the pool table."
7. "If he does that, I'm going to be perturbly upset."
8. "I didn't ask him to deserve this."
9. "I don't want to sue anyone, and I don't want to be greedy. I just want enough money to live on for the rest of my life."
10. "Yeah? I want triple indemption!"
11. "This is in contestment."

MARITAL BLISS

1. "I'm having martial troubles."
2. "Maybe I should have blown my head's wife off."
3. "I'll be in stringent contact with my wife about this."
4. "My wife's got a pursuiter."
5. "My wife wanted to meet a guy in the parking lot, and I thought it was auspicious."
6. "I'm not trying to be abstinent about this."
7. "He's not going to slurk his responsibility on this."
8. "If I have to, I'll go to Family Court, and get an order of filtration."
9. "My wife committed adultery, but that was before we were married."
10. "I will no longer put up with the humility she has caused me."
11. "He's got a lot of money. He just bought a brand new Ford Exploder."
12. "It's a very simple divorce. There's no martial status on anything."
13. "I would like to get this divorce as quickly and painfully as possible."
14. "My wife's in a lot of trouble. She's been using a consumed name."
15. "My husband is now giving me altimations."

CRIMINAL LAW

1. "They charged me with failure to resist."
2. "They forced me into contempt of hatred, according to the Penal Law."
3. "They have to have probably cause to arrest me. I saw it on Hawaii Five-O."

4. "They brought him up here from South Carolina on expedition."
5. "They only got circlestantial evidence."
6. "I ordered a supporting definition."
7. "You are my court-assigned offender."
8. "They dropped it to felicitating a crime."
9. "I called because I missed court and I don't want any issues warranted."
10. "My son is charged with burglary, but it's self-defense."
11. "My boyfriend has been charged with endangering the morals of a criminal."
12. " I believe it's a third-degree mistermeanor."
13. "They said I was driving erotically."
14. "They've aspended my license."
15. "If they want to drop it to imparred, that's ok."
16. "They told me my son was going to be charged with no trespassing."
17. "They gave me a ticket and the car was consfigated."
18. "I let somebody drive my car, they got a DWI, and now my car is pounded."
19. "She told me it would be exploited from my record."
20. "When the police came, I decided not to give then a discriminating statement."
21. "Can't we get a flea bargain?"
22. "She couldn't have been sexually abused. The Heimlich is still there."
23. "I got a ticket for driving without a suspended notice."
24. "All right then. Tell them I want an oppression hearing."
25. "I thought I would steal it in the interests of justice."
26. "He was put on probation, and has to pay retribution."
27. "I need an ominous motion."
28. "I need some public assistance about a ticket."
29. "I could pick the guy out of a lineup blindfolded."

STRATEGY

1. "Isn't there any way you can abstain the receipts?"
2. "I've got a new ankle on this."
3. "I want a preliminary estoppel."
4. "Let's order them to attend an EET."
5. "When we go to court, I can add some coercion to that fact."

ETIQUETTE

1. "I told them: 'I'm sorry. She can't see you today. She's decomposed.'"
2. "They asked my husband and I to dinner. So I figured I'd retaliate and ask them."
3. "We thought we'd do a little something special, and give him a plague."
4. "She's a convulsive eater."
5. "Oh, God. If you would do this for me, I'd be internally grateful."
6. "Sorry. I'll call you back. I spend a lot of time on the potty."

RELATIONSHIPS

1. "She was absolutely rampant about it."
2. "I was so angry, I had to be physically refrained."
3. "I'd have no quorum about that."
4. "I think I have an optipistic attitude about it."
5. "It looks like everything is about to babble over again."
6. "A lot of people have been saying a lot of things, deflaming my character."

7. "He was demeanoring me in front of a group of people."
8. "I felt like he was evading my privacy."
9. "Of course. And now she's being very invictive."
10. "It was his life story. I saw it on 'Biology.'"

FINANCE

1. "I just got the letter of contentment from my bank."
2. "There's a judgment, and now they've guaranteed his wages."
3. "His check bounced. Do I have to detest it?"
4. "I was under the influence that if they backed out, they would lose their money."
5. "I don't have the money. I'm not flushed anymore."
6. "I just got another bill from my wife. Am I reliable for that?"
7. "He spent the money on it, and I think he should be imbursed."
8. "In my business, I have to charge exuberant prices in order to be competitive."
9. "I paid for those things, and I want rebusiment for them."
10. "I've gone through a lot of financial copulations."
11. "I've got a survivor annudity."
12. "Our financial picture is unsecured."
13. "I've got an account that's held as TLC with my brother."
14. "Our assets have been liquified."

COMMUNICATION

1. "He was definitely giving me false convictions."
2. "Please let me know your sediments."
3. "He said a lot of verbal language to me."

4. "He's been bugging me with phone calls, and calling all over Sam Carnation."
5. "I'll sign this, but my handwriting isn't too eligible."
6. "He said he'll conversate about it."
7. "Did you try to call him on his celluloid phone?"
8. "I was under the influence they knew that."

FAMILY

1. "Several people on my brother's side of the family were assaulted for theft."
2. "I had an alteration with one of the heirs."
3. "She simply says to me, quite fragrantly, that she can do whatever she wants."
4. "The woman from child prevention service came over today."
5. "Last year, when my wife's mother died, I didn't get a chance to grieve my tax assessment."
6. "Was your child born in wedlock?" "No. Geneva."

ORGANIZATION

1. "I've got everything right here in this vanilla envelope."
2. "Am I the one you spoke to this morning?"
3. "I know she's got a stototastic copy of it."
4. "I lost my copy of my divorce degree."

REAL ESTATE

1. "I called the bank to get the extract of title."
2. "I know she knew about this, because she had a deeded map."
3. "Twenty years ago, my wife and I went out there and planted thirty sicklings."
4. "I don't have any money to pay condolences to the buyers."
5. "This offer has to be subject to a portable water test."
6. "The building was razzed."
7. "What's this about personality?"
8. "I want this money to be put in escarole."
9. "This offer is only interrogatory, right?"
10. "She's been vacillating on the roof."
11. "They said they would leave the refrigadaire."
12. "They made an offer, but we counteracted it."
13. "Well. About this offer here. Could you do an amendum?"
14. "I would like to exhilarate my mortgage payments."
15. "Please let me know if you think we need any altercations to the agreement."
16. "We're moving to Florida, and we don't have a place there yet. So we've put our stuff in an I-Pod."
17. "It's a case of ominous domain."

PROTOCOL AND PROCEDURE

1. "Mrs. Smith was just on the phone. She just got a straining order."
2. "I want to appear before the residing judge."

3. "If you disagree with this arrangement, a co-liable lawsuit will be brought against you."
4. "I want you to file a partition in the courthouse on this."
5. "This has to be signed before a notary republic."
6. "She denies most of the things allegated to her."
7. "I know. I know. It's in the discretation of the judge."
8. "I could go along with that. I'd have no rejection to it."
9. "I really believe you are going to have to nip this in the butt."
10. "I want to appeal the show of cause."
11. "I'm named as the executioner of the will."
12. "I think that's what brought it to attrition."
13. "Let's hit him with a subpenis."

CLARITY

1. "I pacifically told him not to do that."
2. "I am very froggy on the details."
3. "I'm sorry to bother you, but I'm in the middle of the fiddle here."
4. "You mean I've been working all year under a misnomer?"
5. "I feel like I'm losing a defeating battle here."
6. "I'm not familiar with this. What exactly does it curtail?"
7. "It was snowing, and I ran into a wipeout."
8. "I got a phone call from a person, in conglomeration with other things."
9. "He's trying to stir up a kettle of sour grapes."
10. "I'd like to turn my sorted past into an advantage for me."
11. "Please try to bare with me."
12. "I'm sort of in a pondry here."

13. "He gave the case to his partner. And he was a new partner. He was only three months old."
14. "I hate to throw a curse on the fire."
15. "He was inadvertently not thinking."
16. "I'll go with a tentative expletive on this."
17. "I don't know if will come to frutation."
18. "And that's just one blaring example."

PERSONAL RECOMMENDATIONS

1. "I feel he is imminently qualified for the job."
2. "You come highly represented."
3. "I need a consolation with you."
4. "I'm not going to let her ruin my reputation, mess with my eagle."
5. "Mr. Jones reprimanded me to you."

COMMON COURTESY

1. "I'm in deep regards over this case."
2. "No, I wouldn't enhance you to do that."

SEX

1. "When we were doing our estate planning, we discussed it with our kids, and culled out all their fetishes."

SECRETARIAL SKILLS

1. "Attorney's office. How can I hold you?"
2. "Attorney's office. Happy Birthday."
3. "Good morning. Atturkey's office."
4. "Have a Merry Christmas and a Happy New York."
5. "Is this the person to whom I'm speaking?"

LETTER WRITING SKILLS

1. "Please be advised I'm running out of patients."
2. "The safety procedures have now been impleted."

LOGIC

1. "I don't know if she signed that after her death, or not."
2. "We discussed it, verbally."
3. "Your affidavit is wrong. I don't pay support bi-weekly. I pay it every two weeks."
4. "Things are going from worse to bad."
5. "I worried about it for the next three preceding days."
6. "Oh, my son loves animals so. His main goal in life is to be a compensation officer."
7. "I'm lucky to have a roof under my head, you know?"
8. "The first thing I wanted to ask is sort of a question."
9. "My husband had to de-thaw the pipes."
10. "Yes. I read it. But I found some incorrections."

RESOLVE

1. "When I make a promise, I intend to forefill it."

GEOGRAPHY

2. "I don't know Florida that well. Are we still on the Pensacola?"

A COUNTRY LAWYER'S FAVORITE APHORISMS

A SMALL COLLECTION OF WORDS OF MEANING FOR A WORTHY LIFE

Over the years I have occasionally taken a moment to record a few sayings that have meant something to me. There could have been many more.... It's a work in progress.

This above all: to thine own self be true,
And it must follow, as the night the day:
Thou canst not then be false to any man.

Polonius's advice to his son
Shakespeare, Hamlet

"There's a divinity that shapes our ends."

Shakespeare, Hamlet

"In your answers, always add value to the questions."
Frank Delaney, "Ireland"

"Either we are all God's children, or none of us are."
Sign at a day care, Tucson, Az

"Extraordinary claims require extraordinary evidence."
Carl Sagan

"Watch your thoughts, for they become words. Choose your words, for they become actions. Understand your actions, for they become habits. Study your habits, for they will become your character. Develop your character, for it becomes your destiny."
Frank Outlaw, President of Bi-Lo Stores

"Honor is a thing no man can give to another, nor take from another. Honor is a man's gift to himself."
The Movie, Rob Roy

"To be human is to be beautifully flawed."
Eric Wilson

"To whom much is given, much is asked."

Luke 12:48.

"Wherever you go, go with all your heart."

Confucius.

"You have two hands. One to help yourself; the second to help others."

Audrey Hepburn

"The measure of a society is its obedience to the unenforceable."

John Fletcher Moulton, English judge.

"How far you go in life depends upon your being tender with the young, compassionate with the aged, sympathetic with the striving and tolerant of the weak, the strong and the wrong. Because someday in your life, you will have been all of these."

George Washington Carver

"Life is not measured by the number of breaths we take, but by the moments that take our breath away. A nation's greatness is measured by how it treats its weakest members."

Mahatma Ghandi

"...the moral test of government is how that government treats those who are in the dawn of life, the children; those who are in the twilight of life, the elderly; those who are in the shadows of life; the sick, the needy and the handicapped. "

Last Speech of Hubert H. Humphrey

"There's something like a line of gold thread running through a man's words when he talks to his daughter, and gradually over the years it gets to be long enough for you to pick up in your hands and weave into a cloth that feels like love itself."

John Gregory Brown, Decorations in a Ruined Cemetery, 1994

"Then we sat at the end of the earth, with our feet dangling over the side, and marveled that we had found each other."

Anon.
Seen in a shop in San Clemente, California, March, 2014
(I've turned this into a song for my third album).

"Shared joy is double joy; shared sorrow is half sorrow."

Swedish proverb

"There are three things we cry for in life: things that are lost, things that are found, and things that are magnificent."

Douglas Coupland, author and designer

"People will forget what you said. People will forget what you did. But people will never forget how you made them feel."

Maya Angelou

"In the confrontation between the stream and the rock, the stream always wins; not through strength, but by perseverance."

H. Jackson Brown

"You are the books you read, the films you watch, the music you listen to, the people you meet, the dreams you have, and the conversations you engage in. You are what you take from these. You are the sound of the ocean, breath of the fresh air, the brightest light and the darkest corner. You are a collective of every experience you have had in your life. You are every single second of every day. So drown yourself in a sea of knowledge and existence. Let the words run through your veins and the colors fill your mind until there is nothing left to do but explode. There are no wrong answers. Inspiration is everything. Sit back, relax, and take it all in. "

Jac Vanek

"In the end, we will remember not the words of our enemies, but the silence of our friends."

Martin Luther King

"A rising tide lifts all the boats."

New England Council slogan, adopted by John F. Kennedy

"It is difficulties that show what men are."

Epictetus

"A man should be upright, not be kept upright."

Marcus Aurelius

"Buried pain never gets better with age."

James Comey

"I have had more love in a single day of my life than many people have had in their entire lives."

Me

First They Came

First they came for the socialists, and I did not speak out—
Because I was not a socialist.
Then they came for the trade unionists, and I did not speak out—
Because I was not a trade unionist.
Then they came for the Jews, and I did not speak out—
Because I was not a Jew.
Then they came for me—and there was no one left to speak for me.

Martin Niemoller

"No seed ever sees the flower."

Anonymously on a calendar

"I am the captain of my soul."

Poem, Invictus, William Ernest Henley

"The purpose of life is to discover your gift. The meaning of life is to give your gift away."

Pablo Picasso

"Rings and jewels are not gifts, but apologies for gifts. The only gift is a portion of thyself. Thou must bleed for me. Therefore the poet brings his poem; the shepherd, his lamb; the farmer, corn; the miner, a stone; the painter, his picture; the girl, a handkerchief of her own sewing."

"Gifts", essay by Ralph Waldo Emerson

"I am not bound to win, but I am bound to be true.
I am not bound to succeed, but I am bound to live by the light that I have. I must stand with anybody that stands right, and stand with him while he is right, and part with him when he goes wrong."

Abraham Lincoln

"Freedom is never more than one generation away from extinction. We didn't pass it to our children in our bloodsream. It must be fought for, protected and handed on to them for them to do the same."

Ronald Reagan

"Never give in, never give in, never, never, never, never... in nothing great or small, large or petty; never give in except to convictions of honor and good sense."

Winston Churchill

"The flame that burns twice as bright burns half as long."

Lao Tzu Te Tao Ching

"Some people talk about other people's failures with such pleasure that you would swear they are talking about their own successes."

Mokokoma Mokhonoana

"Be kinder than necessary, for everyone you meet is fighting some kind of battle."

Anon

"People who do really good stuff have flaws."

President Barack Obama

"When I was 5 years old, my mother always told me that happiness was the key to life. When I went to school, they asked me what I wanted to be when I grew up. I wrote down `happy'. They told me I didn't understand the assignment, and I told them they didn't understand life."

John Lennon

"In a world where you can be anything, be kind."

Anon

"Music has charms to soothe a savage breast."

William Congreve 1697

"The fight is here; I need ammunition, not a ride"

"We will not give up and we will not lose. We will fight to the end; at sea, in the air; we will continue fighting for our land, whatever the cost."

"Our weapons are our truth."

"You are being told we hate culture. How can someone hate culture? Any culture? Neighbors always enrich one another culturally."

"When you attack us, you will see our faces. Not our backs, but our faces."

Volodymyr Zelenski 2022

"Tell all your friends that I am kind."

Six year old Catherine Violet Hubbard, gently whispered to animals in her care. She was one of the first-grade victims of the December 14, 2012 Sandy Hook school shooting tragedy in Newtown, Ct. There is now a beautiful animal sanctuary in that town in her honor.

Do not stand at my grave and weep;
I am not there, I do not sleep.
I am a thousand winds that blow,
I am the diamond glints on snow.
I am the sunlight on ripened grain;
I am the gentle autumn's rain.
When you awaken in the morning's hush
I am the swift uplifting rush
Of quiet birds in circled flight.
I am the soft stars that shine at night.
Do not stand at my grave and cry;
I am not there; I did not die.

Native American prayer

"If there were no cost do doing what's right, there would be no such thing as courage."

Mitt Romney, on declaring he will not run again for the Senate

"When a learned man dies, it's like a library closes."
>African proverb, repeated by Charles DeVoll at Clifton Springs Hospital Sept. 2023

"May the sun bring you new energy by day, may the moon softly restore you by night, may the rain wash away your worries, may the breeze blow new strength into your being, may you walk gently through the world and know its beauty all the days of your life."
>Apache blessing, recalled by Robin Allen in a card of encouragement to Liz; Sept. 2023

"At his best, man is the noblest of all animals; separated from law and justice he is the worst."
>Aristotle

ABOUT THE AUTHOR

John E. Tyo, Esq., is a seasoned country lawyer, having served upstate New York for 55 years before retiring in 2024. His extensive legal experience spans criminal and civil trials, real estate, family court, and over 300 appeals. Tyo held chair positions in local NYS bar associations and legal aid organizations, and was active in political party activities. Beyond law, he's an amateur songwriter with two albums to his credit and a third in the pipeline. His book, *Country Lawyer, Last Of A Dying Breed*, reflects his rich legal career and passion for serving rural communities.

www.ingramcontent.com/pod-product-compliance
Lightning Source LLC
LaVergne TN
LVHW021818060526
838201LV00058B/3429